# Peoples on the Move

# Peoples on the Move

Community Research for Ministry and Missions

### Anthony F. Casey

*Foreword by J. D. Payne*

WIPF & STOCK · Eugene, Oregon

PEOPLES ON THE MOVE
Community Research for Ministry and Missions

Copyright © 2020 Anthony F. Casey. All rights reserved. Except for brief quotations in critical publications or reviews, no part of this book may be reproduced in any manner without prior written permission from the publisher. Write: Permissions, Wipf and Stock Publishers, 199 W. 8th Ave., Suite 3, Eugene, OR 97401.

Wipf & Stock
An Imprint of Wipf and Stock Publishers
199 W. 8th Ave., Suite 3
Eugene, OR 97401

www.wipfandstock.com

PAPERBACK ISBN: 978-1-5326-9619-0
HARDCOVER ISBN: 978-1-5326-9620-6
EBOOK ISBN: 978-1-5326-9621-3

Manufactured in the U.S.A.                    08/07/20

## Contents

*Foreword by J. D. Payne* | vii

1. Why Community Research? | 1
2. Culture Learning in the Bible | 10
3. Culture Unites, Culture Divides | 22
4. The Tools and Process of Research | 39
5. Reviewing the Literature and Preexisting Data | 51
6. Site Access and Informants | 62
7. Participant Observation | 72
8. Qualitative Interviewing | 84
9. Data Analysis | 98
10. Writing Up and Applying the Research | 107
11. Special Considerations for Multicultural Research and Ministry | 119
12. Short-Term, Team-Based Ethnographic Research | 133

*Worldview Identification Worksheet* | 147
*Bibliography* | 149

# Foreword

GLOBALIZATION CREATES A PARADOX regarding how we view the world. On the one hand, we are told this reality makes the world a smaller place. Cultural lines become blurred. Peoples move and bring societal change. On the other hand, we know the global population continues to increase. Culture, even in a small community, is not monolithic, and migration is more widespread than any time in history. The world is a big place. In some ways, globalization brought simplicity; in other ways, it increased complexity. The result is an increased need for the church to understand the constantly changing contexts.

While over the past forty years some Christians have come to appreciate the role of research and community studies, many see little value in such work. Few desire to conduct research in their communities. The irony of this unfortunate situation is that many of those people want to reach their neighbors with the gospel, but will often say they do not know how. Yet, God in his grace has provided a tool to assist in our Great Commission efforts—research.

Christians are people of zeal. While this is a good thing, it is not the only thing. The writer of Proverbs notes, "desire without knowledge is not good, and whoever makes haste with his feet misses the way" (Prov 19:2, ESV). The internal drive for God's glory among the nations is to be part of who we are as Christ's followers. However, unbridled passion can take us in unhealthy directions and cause us to wonder why we are not seeing the gospel spread rapidly and with honor (2 Thess 3:1). God in his grace has provided a partner to be wed to our zeal: knowledge. And knowledge, especially of our contexts, is often found through the divine blessing—the tool of research.

We are quick to forget that community research is found throughout the Bible. Moses sends spies into the land to conduct a survey (Num 13). Later, Joshua sends spies into the same land to do likewise (Josh 2:1). Nehemiah was moved to action because he heard the report of the reality of Jerusalem (Neh 1:2–11) and even did some survey work under the cloak of darkness (Neh 2:12–15). When calling people to count the cost of discipleship, Jesus notes how even the people of this world discern their realities to make decisions in life (Luke 14:28–32). Research is a matter of kingdom stewardship.

This book is designed to help you become a better steward for the glory of God among the nations—in your community, across North America, and throughout the world. I pray that you will accept the challenge to go against the status quo and learn how to understand the peoples around you. Such knowledge will provide you with better insight for proper methods of evangelism, discipling, and church-planting.

Anthony Casey has done a wonderful job helping the church in the neglected area of research. This work fills a massive void in the literature. Search the libraries for books on how to conduct community studies for ministry and the results are meager. This book explains the importance of culture and the basics of ethnographic research. It is not written to make you a social scientist. Rather, it was written to equip you for the work of the ministry to which you have been called.

I have spent years studying, teaching, and applying social research methods. One of the biggest challenges involved taking the sociological and anthropological "secular" works, processing them through my theological and missiological filters, and then discerning how to apply them to my local church and missionary activities. It was a challenging process for the seminary professor, and even more difficult for the non-academician. Casey is correct: "community research can be intimidating and many books on the

## Foreword

subject are overly technical." So, what has he done about this challenge? He has written this excellent book.

*Peoples on the Move: Community Research for Ministry and Missions* is a pioneer work. I wish this book was written years ago! This work takes the best information in the field and condenses it into a volume that many people will be able to understand and apply to their contexts. Casey has taken the best-of-the-best for understanding how to conduct community research and made the complex processes highly assessable. This is the skill of a great teacher.

But this book also shows the skill of a great practitioner. What is found here is not a work of theory. This writing was birthed out of applying study to the field. These pages are filled with stories of Casey's experiences in the United States, across North America, and throughout the world. He shows the local church leader and missionary how they can conduct research in their fields that leads to disciple-making. This is not a book of abstract ideas and lofty theoretical concepts. Casey writes to assist the reader for more effective ministry.

While God does not need research to advance the gospel, he often uses it to move his people to the fields of lostness and enable effective ministry engagement. Casey knows his subject and he knows how to help the reader move to the practical. If you want to understand your setting, then allow him to be your guide to such knowledge and application.

**J. D. Payne, PhD**
Associate Professor of Christian Ministry
Samford University

# 1

# Why Community Research?

## Introduction

SEVERAL YEARS AGO, I was passing out invitations to a church event in the community surrounding the church where I served as an associate pastor. I met an older man at his mailbox and invited him to our church and he responded, "Which church? Oh yea, I'm a member there. Brother _____ is the pastor." I attempted to conceal my true thoughts as I responded, "Brother _____ hasn't been the pastor at this church for more than fifteen years!" Clearly, this man had no idea what was happening at this church, though he claimed to be a member. Pastors and ministers may feel like half the community feels this way about their church, but the truth is, many pastors know as little about their own communities as the community knows about their church. Asked to describe the community within a radius of a few miles around the church, many pastors provide a picture that is twenty years outdated.

## The Changing Face of North America

Across North America, neighborhoods are rapidly changing as people move in and out. Over the past several years, approximately one million immigrants were granted legal residence in the United States on an annual basis.[1] Aside from the recent crisis in Syria and resultant forced migrations, the United States is historically the largest immigrant-receiving country in the world, drawing 20 percent of the world's migrants. Currently, 25 percent of the US population is comprised of first-generation immigrants or their children.[2] Aside from permanent residents, another 165 million or so people enter the United States annually for business, tourism, or as international students.[3]

The United States is the world's number-one destination for international students, drawing more than one million a year.[4] China, India, Saudi Arabia, and South Korea are regularly among the top nations sending their students to us. These countries contain some of the highest populations of unreached people groups in the world. Future world leaders regularly study in the United States during their formative college years. Yet, a large percentage of international students are never invited into an American home and report having no American friends.

Additionally, the world is urbanizing at an accelerating pace as people move to the cities for job opportunities and to escape hardships in rural life. This urbanization often means a clash of cultures as people from all walks of life and holding a variety of competing religious beliefs now live side by side in the same neighborhood. Urban church planting and viewing US cities as a mission field is becoming normative, and rightly so. Representatives from hundreds of unreached people groups now reside in the United States.

---

1. "Table 1."

2. "Foreign-Born Population in the United States," 1.

3. "Table 25." Zong and Batalova, "International Students in the United States."

4. Zong and Batalova, "International Students in the United States," para. 1.

## Why Community Research?

## The Foreign-Born Population in North America

States and cities across the United States and Canada are seeing increased immigration and urbanization. Payne notes that many migrants to Canada "are predominantly urbanites and are even more likely to live in a metropolitan area than Canadian-born citizens."[5] Major cities in Canada such as Hamilton, Winnipeg, Calgary, Vancouver, and Toronto have foreign-born populations comprising 25 to nearly 50 percent of the city's population.[6]

The following chart shows the top ten US states with the largest foreign-born populations.[7]

| State | Foreign-Born Population | Percent Foreign-Born |
|---|---|---|
| 10 Connecticut | 503,209 | 14% |
| 9 Maryland | 874,332 | 14.7% |
| 8 Massachusetts | 1,061,461 | 15.7% |
| 7 Texas | 4,494,345 | 16.7% |
| 6 Hawaii | 253,551 | 17.9% |
| 5 Nevada | 547,696 | 19.3% |
| 4 Florida | 3,967,671 | 19.9% |
| 3 New Jersey | 1,943,338 | 21.8% |
| 2 New York | 4,442,247 | 22.6% |
| 1 California | 10,473,630 | 27% |

5. Payne, *Strangers Next Door*, 43.
6. Payne, *Strangers Next Door*, 43–44.
7. "United States—Foreign-Born Population Percentage by State."

## Peoples on the Move

While this type of demographic research is motivating and helpful, it does have its limitations. The census can only determine the country of origin of immigrants and cannot list which people groups are represented in these states. That localized research is much more difficult to determine, is much more helpful, and is largely the focus of the rest of this book.

Payne, in his book *Unreached Peoples, Least Reached Places*,[8] lists the following information compiled from a variety of sources on specific people groups scattered around US cities:

- El Cajon, California is home to "Little Bagdad," with 60,000 Iraqis.
- Of the 30,000 Senegalese in New York, over half are Wolof Mourides.
- The Bay Area of California is home to "Little Kabul," and made up of tens of thousands of Afghans.
- Minneapolis, Seattle, and Columbus, Ohio are home to well over 100,000 Somalis.
- Irving, Texas is home to 5,000 Kurds with Nashville housing the largest number in the country.
- Punjabi Sikhs number 80,000 in New York City.
- St. Louis is home to the largest number of Bosnians, with estimates ranging between 35,000–60,000.
- Detroit has the largest concentration of Arab Muslims (e.g., Yemeni, Iraqi, Lebanese, Palestinians) numbering in the tens of thousands.
- Outside of Israel, New York City is home to the largest number of Jews in the world, numbering in the millions.
- About 5,000 Soninke/Serecole Muslims live in New York.
- Second to metro New York with 60,000, South Patterson, New Jersey is home to thousands of Egyptian Arab Muslims.

---

8. Payne, *Unreached Peoples*, 34–35.

## Why Community Research?

- 89,000 Tamils live in the United States, with the largest concentration in Central New Jersey.
- Albanians (Tosk and Gheg) number 122,000, with the largest numbers living in New York, Chicago, Boston, and Detroit.
- A few hundred thousand Urdu may be found in the United States with large concentrations in Houston, New York, Los Angeles, Chicago, Seattle, and Atlanta.
- Turks are estimated at 378,000 with the largest enclave found in the South Patterson area of New Jersey.
- The Burmese have significant populations in New York, Los Angeles, Bay Area of California, Dubuque, Iowa, and Fort Wayne, Indiana.

God has presented us with wonderful opportunities to reach the nations, as the world truly is at our door. The multicultural complexity of modern communities presents a challenge for effective ministry, however. This book is an effort to equip the church with the skills necessary to step out of their door and into their neighborhood with eyes to see and ears to hear what God is doing. Community research is not something that can be left to professionals. Every believer can build relationships, learn about their own neighborhood, and lovingly meet the needs they discover as they share the life-giving gospel in a hurting world.

## The Intent of this Book

Community research can be intimidating and many books on the subject are overly technical. Christians may feel that if they don't have a degree in sociology or anthropology there is no way they can make sense of the technical jargon and research skills needed to learn about their community. Over the years I have been involved with community research projects in dozens of neighborhoods across America and on four continents. I have taught research methods to hundreds of students and trained many in the church. Over time, people have begun asking for this training in an easy to understand format that does not require several years of academic study. This book is the answer to those requests. I wanted to write something that was in-depth enough to be thorough but still readable for the regular person. In that light, I write mainly in the first person and take a nonacademic format, using few footnotes. I take an applied approach and attempt to show how good research can shed light on real world problems and equip the church to minister effectively, especially across cultures and in multi-cultural communities. Before moving into the main content of the book, it will be helpful to provide an overview of community research as a whole and explain some of the terminology you will encounter throughout the book.

## What Is Community Research?

You will find various names for the kind of research I describe in this book. Some call it community research, others call it neighborhood mapping. The technical name is ethnographic research. This name comes from two Greek words simply meaning writing about or describing a community. That's what we are after—to learn as much as we can about the dynamics of our neighborhood and then describe what we find to those interested in ministry. In our case, we use the research to develop an appropriate ministry strategy for the specifics of the community. We seek to answer questions such as who lives here, what languages do they speak, what spiritual beliefs do they have, what family structures are present, what needs do people have, what resources might already be present to meet these needs, what churches are at work, and what is the most appropriate strategy for ministry?

Community research is both a process and an outcome. It is a process in that it allows you to build relationships with people in the community as you gather your information. It takes time to get a good handle on all the dynamics. Yet, it is not wasted time because often, those people you get to know in the research phase become the very ones that are later integral in your ministry. In a sense, community research never ends because the neighborhood

## Why Community Research?

is always changing. However, after completing a basic survey, you have a tool that can be used for mobilization and training.

I was part of a team conducting research in Iqaluit, Nunavut, Canada a few years ago, just shy of the Arctic Circle. A major church-planting network was hoping to send new church-planting teams to the area but first wanted to learn what they could about the community, any present churches, and especially the relational dynamics between the indigenous Inuit people and the white population. I had posted the fruits of our research in a write-up on my website and was later contacted by a man who had a burden for the Inuit. He told me he had found the research and God has used it to confirm his calling to the Arctic, where he currently lived and was in the beginning phases of planting a church! I was overjoyed at this news. Good research can also help others doing similar work around the world. New Tribes Mission (now Ethnos360) learned of my research and was especially interested in what we found regarding language revitalization among the Inuit. They used our findings to provide recommendations for small indigenous tribes in the Amazon basin who were in danger of their language going extinct.

In my estimation, community research is a necessity for every church, whether rural or urban, a church plant or a revitalization. Many people have an intuitive sense of their neighborhood, but making an effort to go deeper can be of great benefit for the ministry. Additionally, God is raising up a generation of people passionate about church planting and many are moving to new cities as a result. Neighborhood assessment is regularly part of the church-planting process, but many tools are overly statistical or do not provide the depth I want to achieve in this book. Spending time conducting good research initially can save many unnecessary hardships later on. Furthermore, many churches engage in short-term mission trips and utilizing one for community research purposes is a wise use of time. I have been on several short-term trips where we used a team-based approach to research with great success. Ten people working hard for a week can equivocate the research hours a single person may need six months to accumulate. Later in this book we will look more closely at how to do short-term, team-based research. In short, God has already provided you and your church with the resources you need to conduct good community research and formulate an effective strategy for ministry. Allow this book to be the motivation and tool necessary to get you out the door.

## Layout of the Book

At times, I have come across people who are suspicious of community research and the social sciences behind it. They see it as somehow unbiblical and unnecessary. In response to this mindset, I walk through the Bible in chapter 2 exploring how God's people have always sought to be learners in their communities and places of ministry. Effective ministry needs close proximity so we follow Jesus' model of incarnational living and make our homes in the places where we minister. We can learn much about taking the posture of a learner who is fully engaged in his or her community from examining the lives of key biblical figures such as Joseph, Moses, Daniel, and the Apostle Paul.

Chapter 3 provides an overview of culture and its role for both uniting and dividing a community. People relate to one another in many different ways and sometimes barriers exist that create an "us" versus "them" mentality. This chapter helps makes sense of those unifying characteristics that are important to understand for effective ministry.

Chapters 4-10 explore the tools necessary for cultural research. At its core, the process is simply a matter of going into the neighborhood, looking around, finding people to talk to, and then making sense of it all. That's the good news. Cultural research can be a very natural thing that we are already accustomed to doing. However, there is a technical side to the research, especially if it is to be done well and accurately. I walk through each of the steps, explaining what is needed and provide many examples to give a picture of what things may look like.

The book concludes with chapters on special considerations for research in multicultural cities and then a guide to short-term, team-based research. An appendix provides a sample survey that is useful as you conduct your own research.

## Conclusion

Pastors and Bible teachers receive training on how to exegete the Scriptures, that is, how to read them in a way to clearly understand what God is communicating and be able to transfer that message to the church. Biblical exegesis is vital for a healthy ministry. In the same way, we must become cultural exegetes and gain the skills necessary to clearly understand what is going on in our communities. Community exegesis is vital for a healthy ministry. Without it, we have a difficult time connecting with those to whom we minister. My home church had for its motto, "In the city, for the city." No matter where we live, we should adopt a similar goal: to live fully in our community, knowing its people and needs deeply, and equipping the church to make disciples of all nations, even those in our own backyards.

# 2

## Culture Learning in the Bible

### Introduction

I WENT TO COLLEGE 600 miles northwest of my Ohio hometown. I loved snow and cold, both of which Wisconsin had in abundance. I knew I would have to adjust to the temperature, but I never thought I would be confronted with a different culture. I soon assumed the nickname "Ohio Man," though people often asked if I was from Texas because of my "Southern" accent. My first memory of confusion came on my very first night at college. My roommate and I decided to explore the town and as we were driving around, he mentioned he needed to find a time machine. I found this statement perplexing—had I unwittingly been matched with a Back to the Future junkie? Not wanting to appear ignorant, I said nothing and went along. After making several rounds, I again heard the statement, "Surely there is a time machine around here somewhere!"

I was beginning to rethink my housing arrangement when he exclaimed, "Ah ha, there it is." I eagerly looked up, wondering what he was talking about. And there it was. A TYME machine (Take Your Money Everywhere), an interbank ATM network in Wisconsin and the Upper Peninsula of Michigan. I had a good laugh and explained to my roommate how I thought he was crazy, driving around looking for a time machine. I quickly found out I had much to learn if I wanted to be a local and shed the moniker Ohio Man.

Most people understand the need to learn their way around their community. Where are the schools, the grocery stores, the churches? But, in my experience training church planters and missionaries in North America, Christians get suspicious when I talk about the need for cultural research. "Isn't that social science stuff unnecessary? I'll just love people and preach the Bible." Little do they know, cultural research and adaptation are themes that run throughout the entirety of Scripture.

## The Pattern of Jesus

Jesus is the supreme example of one who learned deeply the cultural context in which he ministered. The incarnation at its core is a model of immersion and identification with humanity. Jesus left his heavenly home, where he had been lacking nothing. He took on flesh, language, and culture of a specific region of the world (John 1). He dressed as the Jews dressed. He spoke with a Galilean accent, which was distinct to his hometown. Jesus did what Jews did—he grew up in a locally recognized family structure, apprenticing into the profession of his father, as was common. He regularly went to the synagogue, as his friends would have. He took part in the local festivals and feast days. In many ways, Jesus lived so regular a life that people were shocked when confronted with his true identity. "'Where did this man get such wisdom and miraculous powers?' they asked. Is this not the carpenter's son? Isn't his mother's name Mary, and aren't his brothers James, Joseph, Simon, and Judas?" (Matt 13: 54–55). Before Jesus began his public ministry, he was fully immersed in the local culture, where he truly *knew* the people.

Furthermore, Jesus identified with his people in their humanity and temptation (Heb 2:10–18). He suffered when tempted and is able to help those who are being tempted. He can sympathize with our weaknesses (Heb 4:15). Jesus understood what it was like to live as a first-century poor Jewish man, and this understanding aided his ministry. I remember living in Malaysia, making a Malaysian wage teaching in a local college. One day a Malaysian very familiar with Westerners told me I was the first American she had known that wasn't rich. The first that really needed Malaysians to get by in life. The one that lived as Malaysians lived. In some sense, I had sacrificed and maybe even suffered a bit to live at a lower standard than that to which I was accustomed, but that statement helped me see that I could identify with the failing local currency and many of the economic problems my local friends faced. And this identification helped my ministry.

Jesus, in this same passage from Hebrews, is called our brother (Heb 2:11). The metaphor of family is a powerful one throughout the New Testament. Christians are called children of God, sons and daughters, fellow heirs. There is a closeness and a genuineness that comes from these relationships. This is the depth we strive for in our ministry. My family became very close with a Malaysian family; we were adopted you might say. The husband and wife had both studied at a US university and had known the love of an American family who served as their adopted host family. This Malaysian couple wanted to extend the same love toward my family—to the point that they let us see who their family really was. They invited us to their home for a Christmas dinner but warned me that some of their extended family were not Christians and things might get a little uncomfortable at times. Tongue in cheek, I was told that Americans aren't the only people who have that drunk uncle that likes to get loud at family events. I was struck by their vulnerability as they did not try to hide who they were. We were truly treated as family.

Jesus showed us what it must be like if we are to truly immerse ourselves in another culture. The incarnation is our model for ministry. Yet, we must remember that Jesus incarnated as we never can. He was the 200 percent God-man, fully God and fully man (Phil 2:5–8). We can never fully enculturate as Jesus did. He lived in the culture, but was without sin. Jesus incarnated as Savior. We only point to him; we cannot save anyone ourselves. Yet, to be accepted as a local, to speak the language, to be called brother or sister as Jesus was must be our goal.

## The Life of Joseph

God allowed Joseph to experience severe hardships, but did so for the good of the kingdom (Gen 50:20). Joseph was betrayed by his own family and sold into slavery, yet he ended up in the house of Potiphar, an officer of the Pharaoh and captain of the guard (Gen 37:36). Rather than sulk in bitterness, Joseph went to work learning the ways of the Egyptians. The Lord was with Joseph and he prospered in what he did. Because he understood local customs and did his job well, he found favor in the sight of his master and was promoted to a position of influence (Gen 39:1–6). Joseph spoke the local language and knew how to lead according to local customs. He even took an Egyptian name—Zaphenath-paneah (Gen 41:45). Joseph had adjusted so well that he continued to gain influence until he was placed over the whole of Egypt and given the Pharaoh's signet ring, signifying the ability to make decisions in the name of the Pharaoh himself. Interestingly, Pharaoh noticed Joseph's faith and said, "Can we find a man like this, in whom is the Spirit of God?" (Gen 41:38).

Things did not always go well for Joseph, but we find in him a model for full involvement in a foreign land and people. Joseph did not retreat or isolate himself from local life. He fully learned the ways of the Egyptians, yet never compromised his faith, to the point that the pharaoh clearly saw Joseph's faith in God as the reason he was successful. Joseph served Egypt, an enemy of his people, for the good of the kingdom and God's name and fame were magnified as a result. I know an American who lived in Indonesia and ran a scuba-diving tourist company. This man is a Christian and had been having a hard time connecting with the locals, who were Muslims. One day, as happens all too often, an overloaded ferry capsized and many people died and much property lay at the bottom of the channel. This American Christian volunteered his diving services to the local government and offered to retrieve bodies and recover as much property as he could. The government was so thankful that they no longer hindered his ministry and allowed him full access to any resources he needed. This man, and Joseph, show us that when we fully engage local life and use our God-given gifts, God is glorified and we have a more effective ministry.

## The Life of Moses

Moses grew up in a powerful Egyptian household, presumably speaking their language and receiving a local Egyptian education (Acts 7:20–22). As with Joseph, Moses rose to a place of power and influence among a people who were traditional enemies of God's people. Moses could have lived a life of comfort and ease, but he never used his status as an Egyptian for personal gain. While fully immersed in Egyptian culture, Moses never lost his Hebrew identity. Moses confronted the injustices of the culture, though not in the most ideal manner. The Bible tells us that Moses "went out to his people and looked on their burdens" (Exod 2:11). He saw an Egyptian beating a Hebrew, one of "his own people," and took action.

Moses benefitted from a good education, knew the local language and customs, but retained his Hebrew identity. He lived among the people but still made an attempt to sort out the sinful components of the culture, such as Egyptian privilege over the Hebrews.

## The Spies Check Out the Land

God's people were about to make a big move, and the Lord thought it wise to give them an idea of what they were getting into. God told Moses to "send men to spy out the land of Canaan, which I am giving to the people of Israel" (Num 13:1–2). Moses wanted to know what the land was like, what the people were like who already lived there, and what kind of crops might grow best (Num 13:17–20).

The spies went on a forty-day mission trip, so to speak, did their research, and brought back the report. The land was fruitful and fertile, but there were challenges. They saw large fortified cities and strong peoples (Num 13:25–29). Essentially, the researchers brought back a description of the peoples, and where and how they lived. They produced an ethnography.

It was important to God and to Moses that Israel know something of the land and peoples they were going to encounter. In this manner, they could best prepare to enter the land successfully. While we no longer engage in physical warfare for the kingdom, we do engage in spiritual warfare. It is naïve to cross cultures without first understanding something of the people. Just as the spies in Numbers discovered, so too can we identify bridges to aid our ministry and barriers which must be addressed for the gospel to go forward. Many mission and ministry teams undertake some kind of prayer walking or exploratory trip prior to full engagement of a new community. Such trips help the missionaries learn the best place to live and conduct ministry. Before moving to Kuala Lumpur, I spent time on Google Maps understanding the city layout, train network, and other infrastructure. I consulted with local people on the ground. I ended up deciding to live on a train line that connected both the seminary at which I taught part-time and the university at which I taught full-time. I triangulated housing through an online apartment finder with neighborhoods within walking distance of the train line, moving away from the city center until I found an area that suited my needs and in which I could afford to live.

## The Life of Daniel

Daniel was captured by the enemy and raised in Babylon. Yet, as with those before him, he saw his lot in life as an opportunity to serve God. He worked hard and became skilled in learning, literature, and the local wisdom (Dan 1:17). He excelled in culture learning to the point that his abilities were recognized and he was asked to teach Chaldean literature and language in the king's palace. He did so well that he was promoted to a place of influence and authority. In many respects, Daniel lived as a Babylonian, speaking their language and working in their governmental system. Daniel lived incarnationally, except when it required him to transgress the law of God. Daniel refused to defile himself with the king's food, yet in an extraordinary act of compassion for the local servants in order to keep them out of trouble, made sure he would not lose too much weight or change in appearance as to draw the king's notice (Dan 1:6–16).

Daniel worked in a pagan king's palace, but lived openly acknowledging his God. He did not try to hide his faith, but did his job well and sought to bless those around him. The king took notice of Daniel's faith and his God and exclaimed, "Truly, your God is God of gods and Lord of kings, and a revealer of mysteries" (Dan 2:47). Daniel's faith was tested, none more so than in the lion's den, but God was faithful and Daniel became a great witness among the people.

Daniel models one who learned the local language and customs well, used his gifts to serve the people, and lived openly, acknowledging his God. One of my roommates from college moved to China a few years ago for ministry. He worked hard at the local language, as he was on a student visa for language school. While in China, he did the two things he was good at—working with wood and running. In an amazing act of providence, God used these very two gifts to enable my friend to get a long-term visa and start a strong ministry. He began entering mountain running events and won. Before long, he was a bit of a local celebrity. Here was a white foreigner who could speak the local language and run fast. He was on magazine covers, had news interviews, and became a sponsored athlete from Solomon sports. He used his fame and skills to start a local running club and now has a wonderful platform from which to minister.

One day, he walked in a local wood shop and asked if he could use the equipment. Not knowing what to say to this brash foreigner, the guys said yes. My friend began making high quality furniture and even teaching the locals. Before long, a local

## Culture Learning in the Bible

university heard of this foreigner who could speak the language and make great woodwork. Long story short, they hired him to teach woodworking at the university, bought him more than $100,000 in equipment, and gave a long-term visa. Both my friend and Daniel are the fruit of those who work hard at excelling in a craft in order to become fully immersed in the culture and using their place of influence for the kingdom.

### The Message of Jeremiah

In the midst of the book of Jeremiah is a letter to the Israelite exiles in Babylon. God's people had failed to honor God with their lives and as a result of continually turning their backs on God they were exiled. In a sense, the exile was meant to be a punishment for their sin. God had handed them over to their enemies. Yet, as if a paradox, God asks his people to live in Babylon as if it was their home. He tells them to build houses and plant gardens. To marry and multiply. And amazingly, to seek the welfare of and pray for the city where he had sent them into exile, for in its welfare they would find their welfare (Jer 29:1–9).

God wanted his people to have an anti-isolationist mentality. It would be easy to see the exile as a period of God's abandonment, like a stint in prison that must be endured. Yet, God sees so much more. He wants his people to strive to be a blessing to their captives, even though they are enemies of God. No matter the length of the exile, God wants his people to take a long-term perspective and live fully in the culture. The letter demonstrates what true incarnational living can look like.

One of my friends models this engagement. He had worked with Nepali refugees for years and eventually decided to move into a neighborhood where many Nepali families had bought houses. Now, rather than having to drive for thirty minutes to do ministry, he simply has to open his front door and look across the street. Others in a similar situation have fully engaged their neighborhood. They seek its welfare by mowing lawns, painting fences, and fixing porches. They go to community meetings and speak up about injustices. They volunteer and tutor in local schools. They start and equip others to start local businesses to keep money in the neighborhood. And they share the hope of the gospel in a hurting community. Two of them were robbed while painting a mural on the side of an abandoned building. The incident resulted in them being interviewed on the local news. Why would these people endure such hardships? They were able to answer in front of thousands of viewers, "Because we love God and we love our neighbor. We are committed to this neighborhood because it's our neighborhood. We believe the gospel renews all things and we want to see people follow Jesus and engage their community." Jeremiah and these Christians seek to live incarnationally for the sake of the kingdom.

## The Life of the Apostle Paul

Paul is perhaps the classic biblical example of one who engaged in cultural research for more effective ministry. However, Paul's approach went far beyond simply walking around Athens until he found the statue of the unknown god. Paul knew the importance of understanding his target people's worldview—the lens through which they understood reality and answered the biggest questions of life such as who is God, where did humanity come from, what is wrong with the world, how is it fixed, what is the afterlife, etc. In Acts 13 we see that Paul understood the Jewish worldview and he used a specific strategy to evangelize them by making his case from Old Testament history. He knew the Jewish people had a basic biblical understanding of God, humanity, and the OT sacrificial system so he built on what they already knew and bridged to Jesus. Just a chapter later, we find Paul in a different context, that of a thoroughly pagan worldview. Here, people confused Paul with Hermes and attempted to worship him as a god! Paul appealed not to Old Testament Jewish history, but to God as creator in order to present the gospel in an understandable way to this pagan audience. He pointed out that people needed to turn from their vain worship of idols to the living God, who made them (Acts 14:14–15). In both

## Culture Learning in the Bible

instances, Paul understood the cultural context in which he was working and used an appropriate evangelistic strategy.

Later, Paul spent time walking around the city of Athens in order to better understand what people believed and how they lived. It did not take long for him to realize that the city was full of idols to every sort of god, even to unnamed and unknown gods (Acts 17:16, 23). He then bridges off his observations to tailor his evangelistic appeal to the specific context in which the people lived. Paul contextualizes the gospel but does not change the substance of his message—repentance and faith in the Lord Jesus. Biblical contextualization is simply communicating the gospel in a way that is biblically faithful yet culturally understandable. In order to be culturally understandable, one must know something of what the culture believes.

Paul took incarnational ministry very seriously. He sought to live like those to whom he ministered so as to not present any unnecessary barrier to their hearing of the gospel message. Paul gave up his rights to live more naturally among the people (1 Cor 9:19–23). Furthermore, Paul sometimes worked a regular job alongside those he was reaching (1 Thess 2:9–10). This approach helps the minister know fully the trials regular people go through as they make a living. In some contexts, working a regular job can alleviate some of the suspicion people have of foreigners, especially of missionaries. Working with the people can bring added credibility and respect and give tremendous insight into life in that culture.

My main platform in Malaysia was teaching anthropology at a Malaysian university. I worked with colleagues and had students who were Muslim, Hindu, Buddhist, Daoist, atheist, and Christian. It was natural for me to tell people on the train and in my neighborhood that I was a local professor. My job made it natural to ask people about their own culture and faith. People were not suspicious of me because they understood why I was there. I was paid in the local currency, which was not doing well. I had to work the same long hours as other Malaysians. I made one-third of the salary I would have made in the United States, and as a result could not afford a car or to travel extensively. However, I had something

19

more important—credibility and the respect of non-Christians around me. People looked to where I found my hope as the currency devalued. People asked what I did over the holidays when I could not afford to leave town. While not always the ideal situation, working a job alongside those to whom I ministered proved to be a great vehicle for effective ministry.

Paul did not advocate "tent-making" or bivocational ministry over support-based ministry but used either as the need arose. Whatever his job, Paul sought to learn about the communities and worldviews of those to whom he ministered. He lived incarnationally and contextualized the gospel in order to be biblically faithful and culturally understandable. When necessary, Paul appealed to his status as a Roman citizen. Other times, he gave up the rights of a Roman and an Apostle. Similarly, we may be in situations where appealing to American citizenship is helpful. But, like Paul, we need Holy Spirit guidance to discern the best path. Paul is our model as he submitted to the authority of Scripture and sought to become all things to all men so that he might win some for the sake of the gospel. He was a learner and a lover of people and God blessed his approach.

## The 150 Percent Missionary

We have seen many examples in Scripture where the people of God made a great effort to learn the local culture and language in order to serve God faithfully. As missionaries and cross-cultural workers, we enter cultures very different from our own. We learn all we can about the local culture, but like Daniel, we place limits on how far we go to live as the people. This approach is what Sherwood Lingenfelter calls becoming the 150 percent missionary.[1] The idea flows from the model of Jesus being the 200 percent person—fully man and fully God (Phil 2:5–8). He was born and grew up in a local culture (Luke 2:46). He was fully recognizable as a local Jewish man. Yet, he was without sin. He was fully God.

---

1. Lingenfelter, *Ministering Cross-Culturally*, 24.

## Culture Learning in the Bible

Similarly, we are all born into a culture and one-hundred percent fully acquire that culture growing up. We know by heart the language, customs, family systems, food preferences, and cultural roles common to our area. We like grits, or clams, or lutefisk, or fried chicken. We say y'all or you'se guys. This process is called enculturation and it happens naturally and almost subconsciously. Our culture forms our worldview and shapes our values. We know what it means to be on time, late, or early. We are familiar with our expressions of church.

Then one day, in response to God's prompting, we attempt to minister in a different cultural context. In order to simply communicate we must begin making changes, learning a new language and a new culture. However, it is impossible to fully give up who we were. At the same time, we can never fully take on all aspects of the new culture. We must adjust, giving up some of our old ways and taking on some of the new ways. We become bicultural, a 150 percent person with maybe 75 percent of our old culture and 75 percent of our new culture. This process of cultural acquisition and learning in order to have a more effective ministry is where the rest of this book goes. Such learning does not always come naturally, and certainly comes at times with great frustration and difficulty. But it is possible for those who make the effort. As we have seen, taking incarnational living and cultural learning seriously is not something we have the luxury of avoiding. If we truly want to follow the biblical pattern, we will, like Paul, seek to learn all we can about the people to whom we minister so that we might win as many as we can for the sake of the gospel.

# 3

# Culture Unites, Culture Divides

## Introduction

THINK FOR A MOMENT about the various genres of music common in the United States. As the various genres come to mind, try to answer several questions related to that kind of music:

1. Where would you typically expect to hear this kind of music played live?
2. What would people who like this kind of music typically dress like?
3. If you're adventurous, what kind of alcohol would people who like this kind of music typically drink?

Ready? Go. Bluegrass. Opera. Classic Rock. Hip Hop. Southern gospel such as the Gaithers. What immediately came to mind? I've done this exercise with students for many years and they find they know a surprising amount of information about these contexts, though they have never been to a concert nor have any real interest in that style of music.

What's the point? Most Americans are so familiar with our own culture that we could hear less than three seconds of music and immediately answer all three questions above. We know the answers even if we don't like that particular kind of music. If someone was to invite us to the opera, even if we've never been before, we would have some idea of what to expect, how to dress, and how to avoid appearing like a complete outsider. How do we know these things? Our culture has been engraining these norms into our thinking since birth. Someone from Madagascar could easily answer the same questions about the music in their culture even though you may have no idea how to dress or what to expect if you came to an event playing that particular type of music.

Effective ministry requires in-depth knowledge of local culture. Culture is not just food and language. It is emotional and creates a sense of identity. It answers the question, "Who are *my* people?" Shared culture unites people into a *people*, a community. The same elements that unite one group can serve to distance or divide from another group. Shared culture also creates a "them" or "those people." These concepts are crucial for effective ministry, contextualization, and the formation of healthy, indigenous churches.

## What Is Culture?

Culture is an important concept in humanity as a whole. Everyone has a culture. In a sense, our culture is what unites us as a society. Culture can be defined as a learned and shared system and patterns of beliefs and behavior that give people a sense of meaning. Let's explore that definition more fully.

## Culture Is Learned

Culture is learned; no one is born with a culture. A newborn from Russia is adopted by a US family and grows up in Idaho. Would you expect the baby to grow up speaking Russian? Of course not. They would likely be indistinguishable from anyone else growing up in Idaho. We are taught our culture through several avenues. Those nearest and dearest to us like our parents, grandparents, aunts, and uncles begin engraining values in us from birth. How should we treat our parents? Can we call them by their first names?

What colors are appropriate for boys to wear? Girls? As we get older, the media, friends, school, and places of worship engrain additional cultural values and beliefs about how the world works.

Because culture is learned, we can expect people from different cultures around the world to think and behave differently than we might. I remember my Nepali friend who had a toddler the same age as my son. One day I noticed he had dressed his boy in a pink jumper. The boy had longer hair and a gold hoop earring in each ear. The Nepali dad expressed his frustration to me that everyone thought his son was actually a girl. Why did they think this, he wondered? To most Americans, the answer is obvious. But we are taught from a young age what is the cultural norm for dressing boys and girls. My Nepali friend grew up in a different culture with different answers to those questions.

## Culture Is Shared

Culture is not only learned, but is shared by a group of people uniting under the same culture. A single person cannot make up a culture, by definition. Culture is what unites a people so they think of themselves as a people, "us." Culture is what allows them to look at someone else and use the term "they." When people from different cultures live in close proximity to one another, it's the "us" and "them" that can cause problems. Have you ever heard someone say, "Well, *we* would never do that. We were raised better"? Or, "*Those* people always do _____." Monocultural people might think like that about people around the world. Culture is powerful and shapes our values. We might consider ourselves hardworking and honest and another group lazy and deceitful. The shared element of culture unites us, but those same categories of unity divide us from other cultures. Christians should celebrate cultural diversity because all people are created in the image of God and have equal value. The cultural diversity in the world is in some sense an expression of the creative nature of the Trinity. Christians should not think another culture better or worse than their own, though we often do, even if it is a subconscious thought. We should desire to work hard to learn all we can about another culture, especially if we want to share the gospel and minister among them.

## Culture Is Composed of Patterns

Another aspect of shared culture is the patterns of behavior we come to expect and recognize because we have seen them over and over growing up. Imagine walking down the sidewalk and a man approaches with a smile and says, "Hey, I saw you at church last week, how are you?" You are likely not gripped with anxiety, heart racing, palms sweating wondering how in the world do I greet this man? No, you automatically extend your hand and shake his and reply, "I'm fine. How are you?" You know how to greet the man because of your cultural pattern. How does a pattern work? 1, 2, 3. 1, 2, 3. 1, 2, _. Fill in the blank. Obviously 3. How do you know? You've noticed a pattern has developed. Patterns help you fill in the blanks and know what comes next. Imagine walking down the street in Eastern Europe. A man walks toward you and says hi. You extend your hand. He grabs your head and kisses you on both cheeks. Not what you were expecting. Different culture, different pattern. Those who work cross-culturally need to learn the various patterns for doing life in that culture. If you don't, life will be filled with anxiety as you never know what to expect and are constantly surprised at what you encounter. If you don't follow the prescribed patterns appropriate for that culture, you will always appear an outsider, as will the Jesus you represent and proclaim, and you will likely have little ministry impact.

## Culture Informs Beliefs and Behavior

Where does sickness come from? The answer to that question likely depends on the culture in which you grew up. You may answer that sickness comes from a virus or bacteria that disrupts bodily biological systems. You may even be able to draw the virus in its various life stages and forms depending on what symptoms are present. Someone else may answer that sickness comes from a spiritual imbalance as a result of upsetting the spirits. Your deceased ancestor is angry and has come back to bring ill on you. How is sickness cured? You may answer that a bacterial illness can be cured by taking antibiotics. They place markers on the bacterial cells that your white blood cells then seek out and destroy. Someone else may answer that you must see the shaman so she can divine which spirit you have upset. The cure may be brought about through a sacrifice of a chicken. So who is right? Depending on your views, you may think the other person's answer is the stupidest thing you've ever heard, and the same for them toward your view.

Our culture teaches us how the world works, and then reinforces these beliefs in a thousand ways as we grow up. In this sense, culture is socially constructed. Different cultures provide different answers to questions about life. How do we greet one another? Is the husband or the wife more important? What are the responsibilities of the first-born son in the family? Who eats first at a meal? How do friendships develop? How do we find a spouse? Is dating allowed? What do we do when someone dies? And on and on.

It's helpful to think about perception of reality when we talk about culture. For most people, perception *is* reality, even if the belief is not true. And then people act on their perceptions. I remember conducting community research in a very multiethnic area of Queens, New York. One helpful question was to ask people who they thought was responsible for most of the crime in the area. Answers varied dramatically depending on who I asked but one thing was certain—it was never *their* people who committed the crimes. African Americans blamed the Hispanics. Hispanics blamed the Bengalis. Bengalis blamed the Haitians. And each group treated the others according to their perceptions. It did not matter that I could show a police log and demonstrate statistically which group was *really* responsible for the crime. To each culture, perception *was* reality and this was very helpful to know because they were not likely to respect one another well enough to come together for community Bible studies, tutoring, or really any other attempt ministers might make to reach the people. Only good community research helped me understand the neighborhood dynamics and what united some people under a common identity and what divided them against others in the community. This knowledge eventually leads to appropriate discipleship.

## Culture Provides Meaning in Life

What is living the good life? Is it making a lot of money? It is leaving the world a better place for those who come after us? Is it having a family? Is it following Jesus Christ, wherever he calls? Culture helps us make sense of life and gives us a sense of meaning and purpose. What are we ultimately striving for? Westerners often want money, security, and power. Middle-Easterners may want a large family. Some Asians want respect and honor. In a sense, our culture sets us on our path in life and is the driving force behind why we do what we do. I know many Americans who cannot understand why the local Thai restaurant is closed on Monday and why the Thai family that runs it leaves the country for a month a year. They think about how much money the family is losing. They fail to understand the Thai family pursues different values in life and some things are more important than money. Money is not the ultimate goal in life.

Christians are still bound to some degree by their culture, even if they do not realize it. The Bible should inform our culture and shape our ultimate beliefs and values and perhaps help us see a different big picture sense of meaning than those unbelievers around us.

## Culture Change

Culture is fluid and changes over time, albeit often very slowly. Think about America and what differences in cultural values we have since the end of World War Two. Think about how TV commercials have changed over the years, what fashion has been in, and what is cool.

Is the word "cool" even cool anymore? Since culture is shared, often by a large bloc of people, change can take time. However, there are a few factors that speed up culture change, none more so than the internet. The internet has helped accelerate globalization.

## Globalization

Globalization is the increasing interconnectivity of the world's cultures and a sharing of products, ideas, beliefs, and values. What we call "Westernization" is really a form of globalization. Go just about anywhere in the world and you are likely to find Coca-Cola, McDonalds, KFC, and Starbucks. These products do not come alone and are not neutral. They begin to shape cultural values regarding efficiency, use of time, profit, marketing, and wants versus needs. Globalization goes both ways however, and the West has been experiencing an "Easternization" as well. Yoga is increasingly popular in America. Campus ministries at major universities are increasingly Asian in makeup. White Americans are gravitating toward Buddhist groups. The prominence of non-Western ethnic restaurants has skyrocketed.

Ideas about how to do business, taste in music, and views on democracy and individual rights and freedoms have all been influenced by globalization. The Arab Spring uprisings in North Africa a few years back were largely fueled by the internet and social media. Gone are the days when Americans get off the boat after an arduous six-month journey and step into a completely foreign world. These days, one can be anywhere in the world in less than one day's travel.

Transnationalism is connected closely with globalization. Transnationalism occurs when individuals live and work in more than one country. A businesswoman may be in New York City on Monday, London on Wednesday, and Singapore on the weekend. Transnational people must have the skills to survive in a variety of cultures, and are often a mix of cultural influences and preferences themselves. Travel changes people and travel has changed those who come to America from other cultures.

## Migration

Migration changes people as well. Remember the 150 percent person from the previous chapter? It has been interesting to keep in touch with my Malaysian students as they transitioned to U.S. universities to complete their degrees as part of the American Degree Transfer Program in which I taught while in Malaysia. I remember telling my students that they will never be the same once they come to America. They will return to Malaysia with different ideas about culture, beliefs, and values.

Sometimes, American pastors and missionaries working in America overly romanticize people they encounter from other cultures. That man from China you see at the park may not be as traditionally Chinese as you think. People in migrant settings adopt some type of survival strategy to succeed in their new culture. Everyone is on a spectrum with regard to how strongly they retain their cultural, religious, and ethnic identity from their home countries. Some choose to maintain a clear boundary and live almost as a transplanted plant, still in the same pot. Others make choices to adapt and integrate more fully into their new host culture. Perhaps publicly they act similar to other Americans, but privately they revert to their home language and cultural preferences. Others may more fully assimilate and jettison their home culture. The point is that migration changes people and forces them to make choices about cultural maintenance and expression. Good community research can make all the difference in understanding how people identify themselves, how they relate to others, and to what ministry strategies they may be receptive.

## The Cultural Values Spectrum

Anthropologist Geert Hofstede identified what he calls synthetic cultures. Drawing on the work of others, Hofstede created cultural categories that help make sense of ways people around the world approach different aspects of life. These categories are on a continuum or spectrum. They are called synthetic cultures because no one culture or individual is completely on one side or the other, but lays somewhere on the spectrum. These categories are very generalized and can stereotype cultures or individuals unfairly. Additionally, not everyone from a given culture behaves like that culture in general. Furthermore, people change over time and even respond differently in different circumstances. Caveats aside, these cultural categories are still helpful in giving a general sense of what to expect when we cross cultures or what to expect of someone from that culture who now lives in the United States. There are a variety of names for the categories depending on author. I have singled out five that I find most crucial to cross-cultural work.

## Direct versus Indirect Communication

As my former missions professor David Sills has said, cultures tend to use language for two purposes:

1. To communicate information and
2. to maintain the relationship.

Different cultures place a priority on one of those two purposes. Americans as a whole tend to value face to face, direct communication and primarily see language as a means to communicate information first. We value sayings like "Tell it like it is" or "Don't beat around the bush, just come out with it." Other cultures find this style of communication overly direct and too blunt. They prefer to find out how the person is doing and show they care about the person before asking for information. I experienced this indirect preference first-hand one day in Malaysia. I often ate lunch at a *mamak*, and outdoor food stall common in Malaysia. When I would go to the register to pay the bill, the local man would look past me and not make any eye contact or even acknowledge my presence until I said, "*Apa khabar, kawan?*" or "How are you, my friend?" Then he would smile and reply, "*Khabar baik*" or "I'm fine." We'd have a chat about our families. Only then would he settle the bill with me.

People in indirect cultures feel as though you are treating them like a vending machine if you simply walk up and immediately ask too direct a question. Put in the quarter, ask "Which way to the mall?" and then receive your answer: "Two blocks to the left." Americans in the South or parts of rural America tend to prefer at least a semblance of indirect, relationship-building communication before getting to business. The cashier may ask, "How's your momma and them?" before scanning your items. I'm from the North but lived in Birmingham, Alabama for a time. I found myself getting frustrated in the checkout line at the grocery because the clerk seemed to have an excessively long conversation with every customer. "Just scan the items and move on!" I found myself thinking.

It is helpful to know what kind of person you are encountering in ministry because using too direct an approach can cause you to appear rude, pushy, and only caring about some piece of information that benefits yourself and shows little concern for those to whom you are speaking. It is not a waste of time to engage in small talk first in order to establish a relationship and show the person you care about them. This approach will hopefully ensure a stronger friendship and make it likely you will receive more accurate information.

## Task versus Relationship

This category relates to the previous. Americans tend to be more task-oriented and feel a tension to get the job done and then talk or play. We focus on one thing at a time and want to do it to completion. We see people stopping to talk to us as an unnecessary distraction or waste of time. Task orientation goes hand in hand with direct communication. In order to get the task done efficiently, we need to use concise, precise, to-the-point communication. Not a bad thing, but again, such an approach can appear rude to someone from an indirect culture who values relationship-building. The American orientation toward task completion is part of why it feels so uncomfortable to walk through a neighborhood and talk to random strangers. We are not used to living in a far more community-based society where people tend to spend much more time talking with one another.

You may have heard stories of missionaries in Middle Eastern countries or other relationship-oriented cultures spending hours drinking tea before getting to the real point of the visit. My friend John lives in India and told me how he struggled with this approach and actually had to spend some months building his caffeine tolerance just so he was able to "build the relationship" long enough to talk about the gospel! For research purposes in relationship-oriented cultures, even in US neighborhoods, the researcher can expect to interview fewer people each day as it will be necessary to establish a good relationship before asking questions.

## Individualism versus Group Identity

The United States is a very individualistic nation. We value individual rights, expect everyone to think for themselves and have a personal opinion about something that they are all too quick to share, and see little connection between what one person does and how that might reflect on society as a whole. We don't believe the proverb "a bad apple spoils the bunch." Group-oriented cultures, also known as collective cultures, see the group as a whole before they see the individual. People are not expected to give their own opinion, but often recite the consensus view or that of their leaders. These people are not as likely to say anything negative about their people because they do not feel liberty to stand up as one individual and make such a statement. Group-oriented cultures have a strong sense of identity and place community pressure on individuals to conform to the group identity.

This community pressure can make it difficult for individuals to feel free to follow Jesus. Americans often single out one person, share the gospel, and ask that person to make a decision to follow Jesus, regardless of what their family, friends, or community might think. Such an approach is very difficult for people in these cultures. I conducted research on the Hmong community in Wisconsin, looking at religious change across the generations since the Hmong first came as refugees after the Vietnam War. I found that pressure from the various clans and family units was so strong in the Hmong community that few had left their animism and followed Jesus. Instances where Hmong had become Christians usually occurred when entire families and extended families chose together to follow Jesus. When conducting research in your community, it is important to determine if there is a strong group identity. If there is, you may need to conduct interviews with entire families or with community leaders rather than individuals because individuals may not feel comfortable sharing information. I interviewed a twenty-five-year-old Nepali man once who provided all of the income for his extended family living with him in Louisville, Kentucky. The man's father needed to sit in on the interview, even though he barely spoke English. The father's presence was a tacit approval and gatekeeping approach because it was not acceptable for his son to speak for himself.

## Inclusion versus Privacy

This category is related to the previous. Americans tend to value privacy because they are individually oriented. It's not someone else's business what I am doing, we think. We are appalled to learn of communities around the world that do not even have walls on their houses! We laugh at stories in missionary biographies where the whole native community goes down to the river to watch the white missionary take a bath. We feel intruded upon when someone visits our house unexpectedly. My dad used to get so angry if the phone would ring during dinner, never mind that how could anyone know if we were eating at 4:30, 7:30, or anywhere in between. His point was they should respect our privacy and leave us alone to eat!

More inclusive communities tend to have a lot going on all the time. People are always coming and going in their house and they do not feel the need to clean everything to showroom quality before they allow someone in their home. People are seen as stingy if they do not share what they have with the community. Individual property may not exist as such so if someone sees you have something they need, they will take it and use it. We think they are stealing. They think everyone in the community is responsible for the good will and provision of everyone else. If you have ever felt snubbed at being left out of an invitation to a party or not told about something going on, you might begin to understand how people in inclusive communities feel. Singling out people or families for interviews to the exclusion of others can create tension and problems for yourself and those you choose to interview. A better approach is to follow the appropriate channels and interview community leaders first and then ask who else would be appropriate for meeting.

## Time versus Event

Time-oriented cultures view time as something that can be wasted or used efficiently. We view people favorably who are early to interviews. We see this as showing respect. If someone is late, our opinion of them decreases by the minute. We begin to get uncomfortable and fidgety when an event is supposed to end at 11:00 AM and it is now 11:02 and there seems to be no end in sight. We structure our day according to a tight schedule and get upset if something unexpected comes up.

Event-oriented cultures value the activity itself and enjoying a relationship with those present. It's time to go when they've done everything that needed to be done, regardless of how long it takes. It seems rude to conclude a meeting just because the machine on the wall says it is time. Church services in event-oriented cultures tend to be very long, as people blend worship, fellowship, teaching, and eating all together into one single event. Event-oriented cultures also tend to be relationship-oriented, so it was not surprising to me that after a very lengthy sermon at a Brazilian church I attended, the pastor invited up his friend Hugo to preach another sermon simply because Hugo was visiting and it was the honorable thing to do.

When conducting research in event-oriented cultures, be prepared for people to be late to interviews or not show up at all. It is not that they are rude or do not care, but perhaps something important came up unexpectedly so they needed to take care of it first. Time in an event-oriented culture is not necessarily viewed as linear. It is flexible and can be stretched and molded depending on the situation. Be sure to have other things to do in case you find your meeting postponed.

## Cultural Bias

Everyone in the world has some kind of cultural bias, either toward the good of their own culture or negatively toward another culture. We tend to agree with things in other cultures if they are similar to how we do it in our own. It is necessary to identify our bias for at least two reasons. First, as we strive for Christ-likeness in our lives, we should want to know areas where we harbor sinful thoughts and prejudices. Second, it is difficult to conduct good research if we are overly biased toward one culture or another. We tend to find what we are looking for or paint a people better or worse than they really are. Bias arises in multiple channels so it is helpful to briefly examine each.

### Ethnocentrism

Ethnocentrism simply means placing your own culture at the center, viewing it as right or best, and subsequently judging others based on your own cultural preferences and values. Ethnocentrism can be overt when we consciously demean another culture. Or it can be tacit when we subconsciously feel we are better. Everyone in the world suffers from some form of ethnocentrism. Humorously, one country's name itself reveals its ethnocentric past: *Zhongguo*, which literally means "middle kingdom" or more generally, the center of the world. You may know this country by its English name, China.

Americans may be prone to ethnocentrism in thinking our system of governance is the best, individual freedoms are inherently right, or that we make the best cars in the world. Anytime we find ourselves thinking our way is better, or that we would never do it that way, or that they are foolish, we have fallen into an ethnocentric perspective. Ethnocentrism is the antithesis of the posture of a learner, which is essential for good community research. We must temporarily suspend our opinions and judgment and seek to learn as much as we can about what people believe and do and why they do it the way they do. In the end, we may conclude the way they do it is not wrong, or even right, but simply different. Other times, after a sincere attempt at understanding, we may conclude that something is sinful and needs to be addressed with the gospel. What we want to avoid is coming in with guns blazing and give the impression that everything we find is wrong or inferior. People quickly pick up on this mentality and will likely no longer want to talk for fear of judgment.

## Stereotyping

Stereotyping is really just a cultural shortcut. It is easier to make a generalization about someone or some culture rather than go through the hard work of learning firsthand. Stereotypes are made by those outside of a given culture and, while they are not inherently, often tend to be negative. We think certain groups lazy, or stingy, or immoral, or deceitful. Stereotypes shape our views and, consequently, our behaviors. If we harbor negative stereotypes about a particular group of people, say thinking all Muslims are terrorists, we are not likely to genuinely engage a Muslim as a person. We will feel uncomfortable if a Muslim sits next to us on the train. We will likely filter news and really only hear that which reinforces our established negative view toward Muslims. Stereotyping is necessary, as with our cultural categories from above. However, we should always be aware that no stereotype is completely true all the time, and that people often do not adhere to stereotypes common for their culture. When conducting research, we need to be aware that people may hold negative stereotypes of others in their community, or of us as the researcher, that are not necessarily true. Even so, it is important to make note of these impressions, because as we've seen, perceptions tend to shape people's view of reality.

## Archetyping

Archetyping is a generalization about a culture but one that is held by those within the culture itself. Ask an American to describe America and you will get an archetype. Americans are hard-working, honest, patriotic, and love their families. Archetypes tend to lean toward a favorable view of the culture, in contrast to stereotypes. It is a good idea to ask people to describe their culture and its people, but we must keep in mind that they will likely present a rosy view that may not be entirely true. Still, archetypes are helpful to balance any existing stereotypes we or others may have of that particular culture.

## Halo Effect

Imagine stepping out of a store and someone immediately runs into you and sends your bags flying. They do not bother to say they are sorry or even seem to care if you are hurt. The next day you are at a meeting and the speaker is being introduced. "Our speaker today is one of the most kind and compassionate people I have ever known," you hear. "He regularly goes out of his way to help others. Today, I am proud to present Humanitarian of the Year award to . . ." Your mouth drops when you hear the name. You can't believe the same person who knocked you down and showed so little care is getting a humanitarian award. Surely, they don't know the real person behind this façade!

You have just experienced the halo effect—an initial judgment made based on little information but then extended over the entirety of a person or culture. It is estimated that people take only about four seconds to form an opinion of someone and first impressions are lasting impressions, as we say. The halo effect can go both ways—if we have a negative first impression it is hard to later view the person in a positive light. If we have a positive first impression, we are likely to question anything negative we later hear.

The halo effect can be based on stereotypes we already possess. If we think a particular people lazy and then we see them standing at the construction site leaning on their shovel, we think, "Aha, I knew _____ were lazy. Just look at them." Little did we know that this person has been working hard since 4 AM and is simply taking a one-minute breather. We see only a slice of reality yet make lasting judgments. Our humanitarian-of-the-year winner from above had just heard his daughter had been in a car accident so he was rushing to the hospital when he accidentally ran into you. In every other circumstance, he would have stopped to check on you. You didn't have the opportunity to know the full picture, yet you made a full judgment of the person.

## Conclusion

The point with ethnocentrism, stereotypes, archetypes, and the halo effect is that they happen to all of us. They can all be good, bad, ugly, or likely, a mixture of all three. We need to make an effort to recognize our cultural biases, both of our own culture and those we extend toward others. Failure to do so will bias our research and often lead us on a path toward unnecessary sin.

Culture by definition is a shared sense of identity, something that unites us with *our* people and naturally distinguishes us from others. Increasingly, communities around the world are diversifying, exacerbating this "Us versus Them" dynamic. Effective ministry and missions requires we know something of the cultural dynamic in our communities. What cultural barriers keep people from interacting with one another? Are any bridges present between cultures that we can use to bring people together? Good research provides us with the answers. Now that we have an overview of the need for cultural research and an understanding of the basics of culture and what to look for in our communities, it is time to turn to the tools of the research itself.

# 4

# The Tools and Process of Research

## Introduction

COMMUNITY RESEARCH IS NECESSARY, and thankfully, it can also be enjoyable. In some ways, the process is simple. Walk out your door and into the neighborhood and start talking to people! Things are a bit more challenging, however, when accurate and thorough research is the goal. Good research builds on the skills most people already possess. Everyone can improve their ability over time, yet improvement may not come naturally.

I have coached youth sports for a number of years and have come to realize the first practice is one of the most important. Here I meet the players, some of whom I may know from past seasons, but many I meet for the first time. Every player brings varying levels of enthusiasm, athletic ability, and skill. It is important to assess where each player is in each of these categories. Some need extra motivation. Others are naturally athletic, but can easily get ahead of themselves and not focus on the technical skills required to continue to improve. The last category, that of skill, is interesting. Many players have years of experience, but have not been coached well so their actual skill level is low, or even worse, they have developed bad habits that have never been corrected. A good coach can read the players and cater training to each person's needs and in the end produce a high-functioning team.

The research process works much the same way. Each individual researcher, or team of researchers, begins with varying amounts of enthusiasm, natural ability, and skill. Each can improve in their ability to gather accurate information. Some have developed poor habits such as interrupting people while talking. Others are hesitant to begin for lack of past experience. This chapter addresses the tools and basic process of community research. The main focus is on the researcher him/herself since they are the most crucial component of the research process, and the one that can be controlled. Next, the chapter explores the benefits and challenges of using a research team rather than an individual approach. Finally, I present a brief overview of the community research process itself which is explored in more depth in subsequent chapters.

## The Most Important Tool—The Researcher

My wife is a naturally gifted artist. She can scribble on a piece of scrap paper with a broken pencil and produce something I would pay money to hang on my wall. In contrast, no one has ever used the words "gifted" and "artist" in the same sentence when describing my ability. I can buy the finest materials but will never be able to produce quality art because the most important tool in the process—the artist—is severely lacking! Community research bears some similarity to art in that the most important tool in the process is the researcher. Thankfully, unlike art, good research does not inherently rely on natural gifting alone. Everyone can improve and hone their skill to become a gifted researcher.

### Mentality

A healthy mentality and approach to the research process is important. Good researchers are curious people. They like to know why things are as they are. They ask questions and make observations instead of walking through life oblivious to their surroundings. Some call this mentality the *anthropological imagination*. My neighbor is an African-American professor at a local university. Our shared neighbor used to hang an enormous Confederate battle flag across the back of his garage. I wondered what my African-American neighbor thought about this and whether those two had ever interacted. I had never witnessed them talking. In fact, I had never observed my professor neighbor come out of her house. I wondered why the other guy displayed that flag and if he had ever considered how it might impact others in the neighborhood.

These kinds of observations and questions are important in community research. It would be helpful to know something of their relationship if I planned to start a neighborhood Bible study in my house. Would those two come if invited? If one or the other did not, why not? Multiply these interactions, or lack thereof, on a large scale and you can begin to understand the dynamics and difficulties of multicultural ministry and the need to understand how people perceive and relate to one another.

Wherever you begin, you can start focusing on becoming a better observer. Start to look at everything with new eyes and think of what kinds of questions you might ask to better understand the dynamics. Look at the bumper stickers of cars, the kinds of haircuts people have, that church next to a bar, or the tattoos people have. What questions would you ask these people about their experiences, perceptions, choices, etc.? Develop your imagination and curiosity beyond the "what" to the "why," "how," and "why not?" Over time, you may be amazed at how much there is to see that you just never noticed in the past.

## Researcher Bias

Years ago anthropologists attempted to maintain a stance of totally objective, unbiased observation and research. By and large, that approach has been abandoned. It is now admitted that the researcher never was completely objective and that it was a farce to have pretended to have been so. Because the researcher is involved in the research process as a human being, it is overly simplistic and idealistic to think the research is objectively empirical. The key is not to pretend you have no bias, but rather to identify your biases ahead of time.

Church planters want people to come to Christ. Some begin ministry convinced that the multiethnic church is the only biblical model. Such an approach is fine, but the researcher must be careful not to let this bias overshadow reality in the research. In past research in multiethnic communities, I have found unalike people tend to gather together for their felt needs to be met. English clubs, for example, are often a good way to draw a multiethnic group together. However, in some instances when the church planter attempted to transition the English club to a Bible study, the multiethnic group fell apart. On the surface, it appeared the multiethnic approach would work, but once the material went beyond the felt needs of learning English to the worldview-level issues of spiritual change, the ethnic barriers went up and people were no longer comfortable meeting together. In this case, it was more effective to work with each ethnic group separately. A friend struggled with this strategy because he was convinced a multiethnic approach was more biblical. However, these people were not yet believers and did not have the Holy Spirit so was it too much to expect them to put aside their ethnic identities for the sake of unity?[1]

Researchers must come to terms with any latent racial or ethnic prejudice and views toward the poor, immigrants, the wealthy, and so on. Such bias can skew the kinds of questions asked or cause the researcher to lead the interviewee toward bias confirmation. The key in ethnographic research is to let people speak for themselves and share life from their own perspective, whether they are right or wrong in reality. Let's say a church wanted to research the local neighborhood and find out what people thought of Christianity or even the presence of that particular church. Researchers may have obvious pride in their own congregation that could hinder research if the community does not share that pride and high opinion of the local church. While painful to hear, such perceptions are crucial to more effective engagement and thus are valid even if the researcher disagrees with what she is hearing.

---

1. Casey and Wan, *Church Planting among Immigrants*, 79–103.

## The Tools and Process of Research

A final word on bias relates to the physical presence of the researcher in the community. Your race, gender, nationality, and even physical size may influence people in their perception and response. I have been accused of spying for the government on more than one occasion as I conducted community research. In another instance, my team had divided into groups of two while researching a neighborhood. We were not having much success getting people to answer their door when one helpful gentleman pointed out that people thought we were Mormons and did not want to talk to us. I wasn't wearing a white shirt, black tie, and elder name badge, but that didn't stop people from assuming. We quickly divided our teams differently and had much more success! I used to work at the local YMCA as a teenager. I just could not believe a pastor regularly came in to work out. To an unchurched me, I didn't know what pastors did nor what they were like, but going to the Y and lifting weights did not fit in my worldview! If you are a pastor, you may well have experienced a similar "pastor syndrome" where people act quite differently if they know you are a pastor. Perhaps you would not want to lead with that identification when going about the community. Be aware that your presence may be a help or a hindrance and make necessary adjustments to reduce bias in your community.

### Training

Training is crucial for effective research. Choosing and gaining access to the research location is the first step and can at times be difficult to navigate. Upon arrival, researchers must employ keen observation skills, knowing what kinds of things to look for. Observations lead to in-depth questions and interviews, known as qualitative interviewing. These interviews are perhaps the most crucial component of community research. Note-taking, summarizing, and then interpreting notes typically finish out the first stage of the research process. All of these steps require good training.

Many churches and church-planting teams would do well to recruit a team of people to engage in community research and the entire team can go through a training process before beginning. The rest of this book walks through all of the aforementioned steps of community research. Observations and especially good interviews do not often come naturally. Practice is essential. I'll provide tips under each method in future chapters. The good news is that practice improves a researcher's ability to become a better observer and interviewer. Community research is not something that should only be done prior to entering a new area; it should be conducted on an ongoing basis since communities are constantly changing. Each new round of research builds on the previous and the quality of findings should get better and better.

## Take the Posture of a Learner

A final word to the budding researcher is to always take the posture of a learner. We never arrive and years of experience and even multiple graduate degrees are only steps in a lifelong journey. Community research never gets old when the researcher approaches life as a learner. My kids enjoy reading a biography series targeted at fourth graders. There are books on a wide variety of kinds of people, from Che Guevarra to Walt Disney to Ralph Lauren. I admit I have found myself often thinking "Why would I want to read about that person's life? Their field doesn't interest me at all." However, after reading the book (or usually listening to an audio version on trips with the kids), I have found that every story is fascinating. These books have taught my kids and me an important lesson—everyone has an interesting life if you only take the time to ask.

A common pitfall among experienced pastors, church planters, and missionaries is to feel like they have things figured out. Over time, it is easy to fall into a routine but doing so can lead to missing important nuances of community life. Many people ask the question of their gatherings, "Who is here?" but few ask perhaps a more important question: "Who is not here, and *why*?" Lifelong learners never stop asking questions. Good researchers realize that, like I did with biographies, everyone is important and interesting and everything has significance, if only we have the eyes and ears to explore.

## Consider Utilizing a Research Team

I encourage churches to utilize a team of researchers whenever possible for several reasons. First, the research hours can be multiplied through a team. One person might spend ten hours a week in the community for two months—roughly eighty hours of research. A team of six can nearly approximate those hours in a full day of work. Second, teams are composed of people with a variety of complementary giftings and personalities. Some are extroverts that can easily get a conversation started. Others are more suited to asking good, in-depth follow-up questions. Mixed gender and ethnicity are beneficial at times as well, depending on the community context. Third, work can be divided so more is accomplished. Individuals on the team can be assigned a research category depending on their background, education, and so on. For example, someone with a business background could be assigned to interview business owners in the area. Someone with an interest in politics could interview community leaders. I explore specific ways teams can be used in community research in a later chapter.

It is a good idea to recruit a variety of people for the research team. Pastors, laypeople, older, younger, college students, men, women, and retired people all have unique ways to connect with people in the community and bring a much more well-rounded approach to observations and interviews than a single person or a monolithic research team. Each brings needed insight essential to seeing all there is to see in a community.

## The Research Process

It is helpful to walk through the full scope of a community research project before breaking down the specifics of each step in subsequent chapters. I will use my work with Nepali refugees living in an apartment complex in Louisville, Kentucky as a case study. These were ethnic Nepali who had lived in Bhutan for generations until Bhutan began an ethnic cleansing of Nepali speakers. In the midst of much brutality, families fled across the border into Nepal. Unfortunately, the Nepali government did not want to offer resettlement so the refugees were stuck in camps, some for up to twenty-five years. The United Nations began resettling these families around 2007 and several thousand Nepalis arrived in Louisville over the next five years. The city housed them in primarily three different low-income apartment complexes, one of which was near the seminary where I was a PhD student. I was part of a team helping these refugees adapt, learn English and job skills, and hopefully consider becoming followers of Jesus.

## Site Selection

The first step in the research process is selecting the site for research. It may be one apartment complex, a neighborhood, a village, or some other entity. Often, the site is the area surrounding a church or the target area for a new church plant or outreach. The site must be accessible to the research team. In my case, a number of seminary students lived at the apartment complex and noticed the arrival of the refugees. We decided together to begin an outreach.

## Site Access

Access comes in a variety of ways. First is physical access to the site. Can the team literally get to the geographic area for research? Instances where this might not be the case could be in cartel-controlled villages, private condos, or politically restricted areas. Next, can the research team access the site in a relational and credible way? I once spent time ministering in the Cabrini Green projects in Chicago. I could physically walk onto the properties, but had no relational credibility, so by myself, no one would talk to me and perhaps my life may even have been in danger. In this case, it is vital to have local help to gain relational access.

## Use of Informants

Informants are local people that already have site access and relational credibility. Done correctly, their credibility becomes your credibility. For my work with the Nepali, I happened to visit a church near the complex and noticed a younger Nepali man in the service. No one seemed to welcome him or talk to him so I introduced myself after the service. He was twenty-four years old, had recently come to the United States as a refugee, and wanted to see what the church was about. He quickly invited me to his apartment for a meal and we became friends. This man, Rai, then introduced me to his family and many other families at the complex and allowed me the credibility I needed to conduct research as an outsider.

## Initial Visits

Good research takes time and many visits to build credibility and produce the depth that is needed for effective research and a subsequent strategy for ministry. The initial visit is crucial because it serves as the first impression. The researcher need not take notes or be present in an official research capacity. The goal is to meet people, be friendly, and begin to get an idea of where to start. Here, you may learn something of the daily patterns of life, what people generally do, when they are home, etc. This will be useful information for later research. I had many questions during my first visit and meal with Rai and his extended family. I held back and simply enjoyed the time. I did not want to appear as overly intrusive with too many questions until I had more credibility.

Peoples on the Move

## Participant Observation

We are often blinded to many things in the community we grow up in or in which we are overly familiar. At some point, we stop looking at the world around us. Keen observation, however, is essential for good community research. In its simplest form, participant observation is merely watching and learning.[2] Good participant observation goes beyond mere presence, however, as Tierney notes, it "is not just the collection of data, but a way of thinking about the people from whom one collects those data."[3] People express themselves symbolically through their physical materials and relational interactions. In short, the environment itself communicates something of the worldview of its inhabitants.

There is a range of involvement, from sideline observer to full participant, and each has its place and will be explored in a later chapter. Initially, the goal is to look at everything and make note of what you see. Everything has potential meaning and significance, especially in a different cultural context. When visiting my Nepali friends, I noticed all their shoes were left by the door, the apartment was sparsely furnished, there were a variety of colorful Hindu wall hangings and statues around, the elderly parents did not eat with us but ate afterward. Later, I found out there was great significance to each of these observations. Participant observers look at everything, record what they see, and formulate questions to ask based on what is observed.

## Qualitative Interviewing

The general idea for most qualitative research is to let the data arise from the research rather than beginning with a specific hypothesis or idea of what is going on. Following this line, interview questions may not be formulated ahead of time but arise out of the initial site visit and participant observation. I wanted to know the role of those Hindu works and why the elderly parents did not eat

---

2. Tierney, "Becoming a Participant Observer," 13.
3. Tierney, "Becoming a Participant Observer," 12.

with us. I would have assumed Nepalis, being Asian, would respect their parents and perhaps would have allowed their parents to eat first. I would have been wrong in this instance and have missed an important cultural element. I let my observations lead to my interview questions and found out there had been a death in the family and the custom called for a period of mourning where the parents ate the leftovers from the meal after everyone had finished. The essence of qualitative interviewing is to not only ask the "what" questions, but the "why" behind the what. Good interviewing is successful not in the initial question but in the follow-up questions that seek detail and deep description, often revealing worldview level issues.[4]

## Revisit the Process

The community research process is not linear. These aforementioned steps need to be repeated and do not always follow a set order. It is not as if after a period devoted to participant observation, the research is finished and moves on the questioning. The research is cyclical. Information learned through interviewing leads to new areas that need to be observed. New observations lead to new questions. New credibility may need to be gained in new settings. The goal is to circle around and around until an exhaustive understanding of the community is reached, at least as much as is possible in a limited scope of time. This time is not wasted until "real ministry" can begin. It is often during the research process that deep relationships are formed and many of these friends become new believers and great helps to and partners in future ministry.

## Conclusion

Community research can appear overwhelming and intimidating but broken down into its components it hopefully becomes manageable. Many new researchers feel inadequate but after beginning

---

4. Rubin and Rubin, *Qualitative Interviewing*, 176.

the work they feel a sense of excitement and purpose. As noted in this chapter, the most important tool is the researcher him/herself. We all can develop our skills and good training coupled with a team approach can produce surprisingly effective research and insight into the dynamics of a community. Subsequent chapters explore each of these components in more depth and provide training suggestions and activities to build skill and confidence as the research project begins.

5

# Reviewing the Literature and Preexisting Data

## Introduction

COMMUNITY RESEARCH IS MOST effective when a well-rounded approach is utilized. Such an approach includes both an insider's perspective as the researcher attempts to see the world through the eyes of the community as well as the outsider's perspective of the researcher him/herself as interpreter and analyzer of the data. Both approaches are necessary, as insiders may be overly biased or even blinded to certain elements within their own culture. However, insider views are essential because perception is reality to most people. I once interviewed an African pastor and found he had a strong dislike for Muslims because of some of his experiences in his home country. I asked what he would think if he found himself with a Muslim neighbor. He replied that he would be very unhappy. I found this view hard to square with both Scripture and statistics, but to this man, his perception was so strong that it shaped how he both viewed the world and other people.

Perceptions of "those people" absolutely shape how people interact with each other and are crucial to understand when approaching church planting. However, an outside, demographic approach is also needed to balance the insider's potentially biased perspective. It is this review of outside data that is the basis of this chapter. These resources are normally used to give the researcher a general idea of what is going on along with insight into where to begin research at the local level. Many times, names, places, and events are discovered that lead to later, more in-depth, personal follow-up.

## Reviewing Online Resources

### The Census

One of the most important questions when developing a ministry strategy is "who lives in this neighborhood?" The government census is a good place to begin, albeit an incomplete one.[1] The goal of the census is to survey every single person living in the United States. The results are made available to the public and include helpful information such as ethnicity, household makeup, income, etc. The government database is highly sortable and can be narrowed to state and local levels. Such an approach is helpful, for example, to find out how many people of Laotian background are living in my state or my county. Or how many people live below the poverty line in my area? Ministries may use this data to select a site for future work, such as a county with a high foreign-born population, high concentration of Hispanics, or a high concentration of poverty. The census is a good place to begin at a broad level which is later narrowed in focus.

The census is limited in helpfulness, however. For one, it is conducted every ten years and demographics can shift substantially in some areas in that timeframe. Second, the census is like a flyover of an area at 15,000 feet. One can get a general lay of the land, but it is hard to see specific features. The census does not detail to the level of people groups nor identify geographic proximity of people beyond a zip code. These specific features are most important, however, when engaging real people in ministry.

1. See www.census.gov for access to a large body of national, state, and local data.

## Reviewing the Literature and Preexisting Data

Additionally, there is some bias in the data as some people prefer to remain unreported or they may falsely report information for a variety of reasons. Still, ministries are wise to begin at a broad level with the census and then work down.

## Migration Policy Institute

The Migration Policy Institute[2] is a non-partisan think tank focused on issues of immigration, ethnic and religious identity, and many related concerns germane to pastors, church planters, and missionaries. The Institute researches these issues globally and can be searched via region of the world. There is especially detailed data on the United States that can help ministers identify local trends related to immigration, religious change, migration, country of birth, etc. In addition to statistical and demographic data, the Institute produces a number of locally researched publications helpful for more in-depth understanding of city dynamics and local responses to immigration.

## Pew Research

The Pew Research Center[3] contains data similar to the Migration Policy Institute including work on religious trends in the U.S., social and demographic data and trends, surveys on public attitude related to these matters, and access to the research methodology used for data collection that others can employ in their own community studies. Pew excels in their work on religion in America. I have used their studies on the change and decline of Christianity, Muslim birth rate growth, and minority religious experience as I teach classes, train churches, and conduct my own research on immigration and religious identity in America.

---

2. See www.migrationpolicy.org.
3. See www.pewresearch.org.

# Peoples on the Move

## Operation World, the Joshua Project, and Ethnologue

Operation World[4] is a global prayer resource with information on the state of faith in every country in the world. It is more of a mobilization and prayer resource than an extensive data collection. General information related to population, major languages and religions, and the state of the church are the focus of the work. The guide is helpful to get churches and small groups praying for the nations and more aware of the state of the world.

The Joshua Project[5] is a global people groups database. The resource is much more in-depth than Operation World. Here, one can sort statistics by level of reachedness, language, religion, or people group name. Each page contains detailed information on the people group along with links to any available resources such as Bibles or audio Bibles, storysets, and mobilization tools in the language of the people group.

Ethnologue[6] is a product of linguistic experts at SIL and contains data on more than 7,000 languages. Data can be sorted via language, country, region, etc. In all, these three resources are best used for broad research, prayer, and mobilization. For example, churches can select a people group or region of the world to begin focus and potentially take a vision trip to that area to consider long term investment in gospel work.

## Peoplegroups.info

Peoplegroups.info[7] is a collaborative work between Southern Baptist entities the North American Mission Board (NAMB) and the International Mission Board (IMB). The goal is to provide a detailed data set of people groups across North America. It's estimated there may be around 571 unreached people groups with

---

4. See www.operationworld.org.
5. See www.joshuaproject.net.
6. See www.ethnologue.com.
7. See www.peoplegroups.info.

representatives in North America.[8] Peoplegroups.info is like the Wikipedia of people groups. Data is user-entered and localized. Much is available to the public, but setting up an account with the website allows the user more in-depth data such as specific locations of peoples in a city and efforts of local churches to engage with these peoples. Some cities and areas have more data than others, so this resource may or may not be helpful to your area. However, the fruits of your own local community research can be added to the database to continue to enlarge its reach and usefulness.

## Local Government Websites

Many cities have a local government website that may be helpful for those seeking to reach the peoples of the city. I used to live in Louisville, Kentucky, which had a very helpful website with specific sections geared to the international and refugee population in Louisville. Simply finding immigrant groups can sometimes be a challenge and the government website was of great help. It had a welcome page for refugees and listed many resources, local grocery stores, English as a Second Language centers, community centers, libraries, and other events specifically for new arrivals. I simply attended many of these events and met refugees that I otherwise would not have known about. The benefit of local government is hopefully obvious—some of the resources mentioned above are too general to be helpful at the neighborhood level, but a local government site can direct the researcher to "street level" research sites.

## State and Local News Articles

Many entities send reporters to write feature articles on immigrant groups and religions found locally across the country. I have an ongoing research project with the Hmong of Central Wisconsin and have used articles in *The Atlantic* along with many local

---

8. Payne, *Pressure Points*, 8.

Wisconsin news outlets to fill in details on immigration history, cultural identity, religious change, and cultural centers and events related to Hmong and Laotians living in Wisconsin. These articles have helped me find other specialists in the field whom I have emailed and interviewed, as well as names of local Hmong leaders in school districts, city council boards, and Hmong churches. It is always a good idea to do an internet search of your target people or community using a variety of search strings and see what comes up. These resources are a great place to begin to focus specific research you will then conduct yourself.

## Community Resources

Aside from internet resources, which are increasingly available these days, there are often a variety of local community resources the researcher would do well to visit before beginning in-depth community research. Local entities are run by experts in the field and are useful for building relationships, networking, and narrowing the research to what is most helpful for the project goals. Several places may be sought out.

### Libraries

Local libraries, especially in multiethnic and immigrant communities, are very helpful. Not only do they contain the obvious resources such as books, news and journal articles, and access to databases, they are often hubs for community events. I used to regularly visit the local library near my neighborhood in Birmingham, Alabama because I could always find numbers of immigrants there, ESL classes, and many other events created specifically for new immigrants. The librarians had relationships with these people and were helpful in connecting me to families. Libraries often have an information board where people can tack up advertising for all sorts of things. Here, I found dates, places, and times of many events I attended to meet immigrants. Additionally, many

## Reviewing the Literature and Preexisting Data

churches post their own events, furniture sales, ESL classes, driving help, and so on that immigrants desire to attend.

Libraries are fairly neutral and welcoming places for people to meet. This is important for some immigrants, as they may feel uncomfortable visiting churches or possibly even the private homes of others. Christians might consider volunteering at a local library or hosting events helpful for immigrants. It may sound silly at first, but I hear again again the difficulty for churches to physically find pockets of unreached people groups in their communities. Local libraries are a great place to begin and then follow the relational networks of people that extend out from these centralized hubs that gather unalike people.

## Cultural Centers

A few years ago I was driving back to my college with a group of students. We were returning after a visit and great meal with several members of the local Turkish community. I asked the students in my car what they thought of our visit. All expressed a variety of emotions and I found it was the first time any of these students had personally met a Muslim. The students were amazed at the hospitality and welcome we received at the local Turkish cultural center. It is possible to live in a city with a substantial Muslim population, as we did, and still never personally meet anyone from that community! Many cities have cultural centers that are great places to make initial connections, build relationships, and learn about that particular population in the community.

A quick internet search may reveal a number of cultural centers in your area. Often, these centers are established by locals living in the area as a place to connect with each other and celebrate their cultural background. Immigrants in multicultural cities often feel a pull from a variety of sources that can begin to erode their cultural and religious identity. Over time, it becomes exhausting to live in the midst of speaking second and third languages and adapting publicly to the dominant culture. At the cultural center, you can be the real you! It's as if your soul's battery has reached the low-level warning and needs a recharge. At the center, everyone speaks your language, they know your cultural heritage, and they affirm your right to be you in the midst of a multicultural world. Hence, cultural centers tend to gather specific immigrant groups from all over a geographic region.

Cultural centers are designed to promote the ethnic group in the community as well. The Turkish center I regularly visited hosted cultural events and religious dialogues between Christians and Muslims. They invited local government officials, police, and even FBI and Homeland Security officials to demonstrate, yes they were Muslims, but they wanted to promote peace in the city. Essentially, they wanted to dispel any notions that these Turkish Muslims were terrorists. What a great opportunity for local churches to meet and learn about the community! As with libraries, cultural centers are good places to meet new immigrants, build relationships, learn about the community, and then bridge off their networks to gain access to their neighborhoods, homes, and other events.

## Places of Worship

I have been in a number of mosques, Hindu and Buddhist temples, Sikh gurdwaras, and other places of worship in many immigrant communities. Again, the main goal in beginning community research is physically finding people, and places of worship are great places to begin. There are several things to keep in mind, however. First, many adherents of world religions do not visit a place of worship with any regularity. Thus, you are likely to only find a small segment of the total population here. Second, I visit places of worship primarily to learn about the local religious community and not to enter into any religious dialogue. I do not find these dialogues or debates fruitful in many instances. Often, the leaders of these mosques and temples are well-prepared to debate and are not necessarily interested in hearing what I have to say about my religion. In many cases, they also receive a steady stream of Christian evangelists so they may already be dreading your visit, unless you make clear up front what you are there to do. Third, keep in mind any cultural etiquette that needs to be followed when entering these places of worship. I'll spare the several horror stories I have witnessed!

My advice is to call the house of worship and schedule a visit ahead of time. Simply dropping by unannounced does not often prove helpful. Many times, the community will prepare a meal for you to express welcome and hospitality. I am always clear up front regarding the purpose of my visit. Typically, I go to learn more about the local community and ask questions about their immigration history, why they came, where they live, what kinds of jobs they do, what their hopes are for the future, and what needs they may have. You might then invite someone to your own house for a meal. I find such an approach more fruitful than inviting the person to church.

Again, I primarily use visits to places of worship as a beginning point to get in physical contact with the religious community and build relationships that carry on outside, preferably in their house or my house. When I lived overseas I did not visit any places of worship. Simply put, I did not need to in order to meet people because they were all my neighbors at my apartment complex. I did not have to drive anywhere to meet Muslims. I simply had to walk out my door.

## Local Universities

There are more than one million international students studying in the United States and the top five sending countries are, in order, China, India, South Korea, Saudi Arabia, and Canada. Vietnam follows a close sixth.[9] Four of these six countries have large numbers of unreached people groups. The United States is the number-one destination in the world for international study and subsequently, universities are great places to meet and minister to students. Nearly every college and university has at least some international students. A quick search of the school's website often reveals ethnic

---

9. Zong and Batalova, "International Students in the United States," Table 3.

clubs, ESL services, and other entities that gather international students. Other schools have weekly lunches designed to connect international students to Americans. Many schools have campus ministries that reach out to internationals as well.

Contact one of these places and see if you can attend a meeting, serve food, or provide a helpful service like English tutoring. Be sure to keep in mind any campus security policies regarding access, but even on tightly controlled campuses, an invitation from a student is all that is necessary to gain access. I have served on campuses in many capacities over the years and have seen much fruit come as a result. I often invite students to stay at my home over Thanksgiving, Christmas, or spring breaks and had one Nepali student stay with me for about six weeks one summer. We cook food together, watch movies in their language, talk about all sorts of things, and visit any tourist spots within driving distance. I've greatly enjoyed using my home in these capacities.

## Ethnic Restaurants and Grocery Stores

Immigrant communities often generate ethnic restaurants and grocery stores. There are not many Chinese in the city where I now live, but there is a nice Chinese grocery store that I frequent. I've gotten to know the owners and their family and they have helped me get connected to other Chinese families in the area. In many cases, restaurant workers are new immigrants and can feel isolated from their own families and the community in general. Both restaurants and groceries are great places to build relationships, care for people, and learn more about the ethnic community.

A strategy I often employ when visiting groceries is to have a few dishes in mind ahead of time, go in and introduce myself, and ask if someone could help me find the ingredients for the recipes. If things go well, I have even invited the worker to my house to help me cook! I take the time in the store to ask about their families, time in the city, hopes and dreams, and any needs with which I might be able to help. A similar strategy can be used in an ethnic restaurant. There is a Middle Eastern restaurant owned by a man from Jordan where I live. A friend of mine has a very good relationship with the owner and they spend a lot of time together. We happen to have an Arabic studies program at my university and we have invited the owner to help with the program, practice Arabic with our students, and share about Arab culture. In short, ethnic restaurants and groceries are another great place to connect with internationals in the community.

## Using Locally Gathered Data

As I've mentioned above, my main purpose for looking at preexisting data is to learn something about the community I'm researching to find names and places to follow up with physical visits. It's helpful upon first arrival to have some idea of the people's background and already have a few initial questions in mind. It really can be difficult to physically find people so online research is a good place to start.

The physical sites are my second stop in the beginnings of a full community research project. I go to where people naturally gather and feel comfortable meeting me. I build rapport, ask questions about the community, and invite and hopefully receive an invitation to homes where I can follow up and go deeper. Most immigrants are well-connected to others in their community so they can connect me to their larger network. Such an approach is vital in communities without large ethnic enclaves that naturally gather people. Remember that good research takes time, contains many steps, and requires much follow-up. The first step is simply finding people with whom to talk and the resources and places listed in this chapter are great places to begin.

# 6

## Site Access and Informants

### Introduction

"It's either drugs or Jesus," she said. "What?!" was my obvious reply. As she narrowed her gaze, she replied, "There are only two reasons people come to the projects from outside communities. Drugs or Jesus. And one of those can get you killed if you're not careful." I spent several weeks many years ago working in the Cabrini-Green projects in Chicago. These were some of the most dangerous projects in the country and have since been demolished. Thankfully, we had a member of the local community who had grown up in the projects and could use her credibility to both help us gain access to the buildings but also stay safe while we were there. In fact, she likely saved us from who knows what fate when we attempted to go into one building and the teenager standing guard outside said he suggested we come back another time. Our local informant asked why and the man replied that the gang who controlled the building was about to shut off all electricity and beat and rob anyone who was in the stairwells of the fifteen-story facility.

Not all locations are as difficult or dangerous to access as these projects, but there are useful guidelines for anyone seeking to go on site for community research. The first point to consider is the selection of and entry to a specific location. Crucial to access and effective research is the reliance on locals who already have knowledge and credibility of the area. These local experts are commonly called informants. Good community research relies on a network of locals who become partners in the research and, hopefully, beneficiaries of the application of the research in the future.

## Site Access

It may be overly obvious, but it is difficult to carry out research if the researcher cannot physically access the site. It is not always as easy as simply parking a car and walking around. Several things must be considered to help the research be effective. Care must be taken for site selection, initial entry, and the building of credibility. Together, these concerns will help produce fruitful research.

### Site Selection

One of the first things to consider when conducting a research project is how much geographic area can feasibly be covered. There are at least two major ways to divide a project, which I'll introduce here but cover in more depth in chapter 12. The first is a specific geographically bound area. This may be a named neighborhood, a zip code, a certain radius around a church, or something more specific like a certain apartment complex. The second option is to choose a specific people group or population segment such as "internationals" and seek to find as much information about them as possible. Here, individuals or families representing the research focus may be spread over a geographic area much too wide to cover in-depth. In this case, the researcher looks for specific cultural connecting points like those mentioned in the previous chapter and builds a relational network from there.

Whatever the focus, the researcher or team needs to be able to physically enter the community to conduct participant observation and qualitative interviews. In many cases, entry is not a problem. One can simply walk about the neighborhood or visit local shops. In other instances, special permission may be needed. An example may be that a researcher wants to visit a local school with a large immigrant population and talk with teachers and counselors about the dynamics and needs of the community. Talking with a principle ahead of time may be all that is required. In other instances, entry may be more difficult. A friend was ministering in a number of rural villages in Ethiopia and on several occasions, locals threw rocks at him as he attempted to enter the village. He needed the permission of the local chief to be allowed access.

Perhaps only a few sites may be on the radar for a visit at the beginning of the project. Often, as the work progresses, more sites come to the attention of the researcher and need to be considered. One cannot research everything so it is wise to select a few sites that are most crucial to the goals of the research project. Clearly, a site must be accessible, but there are a variety of ways to accomplish the task even if rebuffed at first.

## Entry

Initial entry carries the adage that first impressions are lasting impressions. Care must be taken to follow proper protocols and not create unnecessary offense. For example, it may not be proper for women to enter a mosque alone to meet with an imam. A team of men may be threatening to moms at a playground. Common sense prevails in most instances, but it is a good idea to ask someone local and trusted what should be considered before making the initial visit to a site. Procure the proper credentials, badges, escort, or whatever else is needed. Make a good impression and avoid drawing suspicion, though sometimes the latter is unavoidable.

The initial entry is geared toward making a good impression and developing rapport and relationship, not engaging in vigorous note-taking. Look around, talk to people, and begin to get an idea of what's going on. Have a plan to tell people who you are, why you are there, and what you're doing. People are often suspicious of unknown people. In these instances I defer to the plain truth and not some veiled cover story.

## Site Access and Informants

For example, I was part of a research team tasked with writing an ethnography and recommendation for church planting in the city of Iqaluit, Nunavut, Canada. The city was half Inuit and half Anglo Canadian. Locals were suspicious of researchers because the town had been nearly exhaustively studied by anthropologists. People felt that researchers did not care about them and only wanted to further their own careers or PhD dissertations. We were receiving a rather cold response from locals until we learned of the extraordinary suicide rate, depression, and overall difficulties of life in a region that is frozen and dark six months of the year. I began telling people we wanted to know what life was like here, what challenges people faced, and what their hopes and dreams were because we were going to use this information to send church planters with the lifegiving, hope-inspiring gospel. These church planters were planning to stay long term and invest in the community and its future. I found that such an honest approach helped relax people and show that I was not planning to simply use them for my own gain, but with the aim of bettering their community.

Initial entry is the beginning of a long process of repeat visits. Don't try to do too much at first. Simply being seen can ease the path for future visits. Make mental notes of what is going on and who you might talk with next time. Introduce yourself and begin to get information from contacts. Ask people where you should visit and who you should talk to that knows a lot about the community. What days of the week and times of day are people around? After leaving, make a note of what you can remember and then make a plan for the next visit.

## Credibility

Long-term effective research relies greatly on the credibility the researcher is able to gain with the people. The most helpful information typically comes after many hours have been spent and much tea has been drunk. In many communities, credibility is not given based on one's title, degrees, or accomplishments. It is based on who you know. Credibility is gained over time as people become comfortable with your presence. My favorite part of community research is simply spending time with people. In this way, the researcher builds his or her own relational credibility but there is another crucial component—that of bridging off the credibility that locals already have. Their credibility becomes your credibility. Who you associate with matters and the process of gathering locals to introduce you is essential for good research. The formal term for these local helpers is cultural informants.

## Using Cultural Informants

Local informants are perhaps the most crucial and most helpful piece of community research. Researchers tend to be outsiders in the community, but even if people are conducting research around their own churches, it is helpful to bring along those who live in different places and have different backgrounds and perspectives than the researchers themselves.

### Need

Several years ago I was part of a research team tasked with gathering information about unreached people groups in London, England. This particular day I was in a neighborhood with quite a number of Afghans. I had with me a Pakistani Christian who had lived in the area for several years. We went into a dry-cleaning business owned by an Afghan refugee. We all spoke English so we began asking this man about his journey to London. The story was gripping and was going well until the man stopped talking, looked at us, and then said something to our Pakistani helper in Pashto, a language they shared but I did not. Twenty seconds later, the Afghan man continued in English and gave us great information about the Afghan community in that part of London. Upon leaving the dry cleaners, I asked the Pakistani what the man had said in Pashto. The replay came, "Oh, he wanted to know if you were trustworthy and if he could share more freely about the community without fear of the information used to harm the refugees. I told him you were friends and were trustworthy."

This is a great example of the need of using local informants who already have relational credibility in the community. Alone, I could have gathered some useful information, but bringing along this Pakistani man who was familiar to many in the community made all the difference in the quality of information people were willing to share. It takes a long time to build credibility and the best way to start is by using local informants. When chosen well, they will open doors to information and possibly keep you safe in a way that may never happen if you were to go at it alone.

## Who to Consider?

There are several ways to go about recruiting local informants. In the case above, this Pakistani man was already known to the missionaries for whom I was conducting the research. He was basically assigned to our research team and turned out to be of great help. In other cases, you may not know who can help until you arrive on the site. Depending on the context, several people may be eager, maybe too eager, to help. One must choose wisely. People of good standing are the best choice. The credibility of your informant will be transferred to you, so if you choose a helpful person who turns out to be the local scoundrel, you'll have his credibility—bad credibility!

The key is to let people know what you are doing and based on the response, consider if they might be helpful. Don't make any promises about paying them, at least at first. You want to identify someone who has access to the places and people with whom you want to talk. They may be able to open doors you alone cannot. I had an interesting experience with this approach when researching the community in Iqaluit, Nunavut, Canada. On the plane ride from Ottawa to Iqaluit I happened to sit next to an Anglo man named Hugh. I found out Hugh had lived in Iqaluit for twenty years but now lived in Ottawa. He seemed to know everyone of significance in Iqaluit and after I told him a little of what we were hoping to do, he said just drop his name and we should be able to meet those we needed to meet. A day or two later I was attempting to get access to the city council leader but was rebuffed. I decided to let them know that I "know" Hugh. "You know Hugh?" they asked. "Ok, just a minute, I'll go get the councilman." Now, I didn't actually *know* Hugh, but it was enough to say we had sat by each other on the plane and that Hugh wanted to help with the research. While there are advantages to using someone of high local significance, such a person can create hindrances as well. Their presence or name might cause people you are trying to talk with to withhold information out of fear of repercussions or they may even think you are some kind of spy this powerful person has sent to get others in trouble.[1]

It is likely necessary you'll want to use several informants depending on the context. You may need people with different language abilities, different ages, or different professional backgrounds to help you access people and places in those spheres. The key is to genuinely see informants as partners in the research and not just helpful accessories. These folks are the local experts and you are not. Let them know as much. They can become part of the research team and enjoy a real vested interest in the outcome of the project for the good of their community.

## Friendship

Research projects may last anywhere from one day to many years. Deep relationships can be formed between researchers and local informants. Such relationships are a natural outcome of spending a lot of time together, but also form out of a deepening shared investment in the outcome of the research. Several things may be considered related to friendships with informants.

In general, I do not advise paying locals to help with research. People are sometimes paid on large-scale projects but usually the context is for academic research or marketing research conducted

---

1. Fetterman, *Ethnography*, 34.

by large companies. Payment changes the dynamics of the relationship. In some instances, the lure of money can draw people who may not be a good fit but they might exaggerate their connections and abilities in order to get a job. At the same time, good research takes a lot of time so be sure to not expect too much commitment from a local person. You may be taking them away from a paying job for a time. The best approach is to be open and honest and always give informants an easy way out if they find the commitment too much. Additionally, I have never been paid for the research I've conducted. I see it as a ministry and service to the church and the work has always been done in the context of local churches or mission agencies.

In some instances, friendship between researchers and informants may lead to bias on the part of the informant. Informants may want to please their friends or possibly withhold information that makes the community look bad. Researchers must use discernment in these instances and if it seems a friendship has somehow affected the quality of the research, the researcher may continue the friendship but not the use of the particular person as a key informant, or at least more wisely consider the information they provide.

## Informant Bias

Informants are helpful because they already have local connections, rapport, and knowledge. However, the best use of informants is to help the researcher connect to others who also have local knowledge and then open relational doors to get access to these people. Qualitative research is best done through a verification process called triangulation which involves confirming accounts through a variety of sources. Thus, even if very knowledgeable, informants should not themselves be the sole source of information, howevermuch help they may want to be.

As part of the project I worked on in London I spent time in neighborhoods with a number of Brazilian immigrants. The European Union had recently passed a policy where people who could prove their heritage to someone from an EU country to within five generations could attain a work permit and work in any EU country. Many Brazilians had Italian heritage and so had moved to places like London for a time to work. The agency for which I was conducting research wanted to find Brazilian Christians and mobilize them to engage with other immigrants in London from unreached people groups. I had with me a Brazilian Christian who was eager to help us connect and mobilize other Brazilians—in many ways a great local informant. He spoke Portuguese and knew a lot about the local community. Problems arose, however, when this man wanted to tell us everything he knew and make comments on or correct what other Brazilians were telling us. I remember him stating on one occasion, "Why do you want to keep going into these shops? Everyone is going to tell you the same thing." The reason we wanted to "keep going into these shops" was because we were triangulating data and looking for any nuances or differences in experience and perspective that might be helpful. I did not want our research to be biased by this one man's opinions and experiences, even though he was very knowledgeable.

A final word on bias is the caution that locals may hesitate to reveal things about their communities that paint them in an unfavorable light. Equally troublesome are those who paint an overly favorable picture of their community. I experienced this phenomenon regularly while living in Malaysia. Many from the Malaysian Chinese community described their people much more favorably than I had personally experienced. At the same time, they on occasion spoke overly poorly of other ethnic groups in the country. Both perspectives were biased and too stereotypical to be of use, other than giving me insight that this is how many Malaysian Chinese view life, which is actually a helpful realization! Experience in research helps researchers to begin to suspect when bias is occurring and make any needed corrections with informants. I had to be very clear with my Brazilian friend that we needed to keep asking the same questions to everyone in order to see if there were any anomalies in the community and why this approach was important. He understood and we carried on.

## Conclusion

Community research cannot occur without the selection of a site and subsequent access to that site. The inclusion of local informants is integral to the process, giving the research team ideas, credibility, and access. Site access, while the first in a long list of steps in community research, is important to ensure the vitality of the project from start to finish. Credibility is key and the process presented in this chapter should help the researcher build on a solid foundation as the real work of community research begins.

# 7

# Participant Observation

## Introduction

COMMUNITY RESEARCH WORKS BEST when approached from both an insider's and an outsider's perspective. No one is able to be totally objective, but the researcher is often the outsider who can survey the land, take note of what is there and what is not there, and then find out how insiders use and interpret their culture. Culture, social status, and ethnic identity influence how different people assign different meaning to the same external event. Take for example a police officer as your neighbor. In many white American communities, people might take comfort having an officer as their neighbor. After all, the police are trustworthy and there to "serve and protect." Such a perspective was not shared by my neighbors in Malaysia. It is estimated that up to 90 percent of the police in Malaysia are corrupt in some way and most people do not like the police and would prefer not to have one as their neighbor. The difficulty for the researcher is how to even think to ask such a question if the presupposition is not a regular part of the researcher's culture.

Participant observation and qualitative interviewing go together, and many times are intertwined and not set in a strict chronological order. However, it is best to focus on the tool of participant observation first because when totally new to an area, the researcher may not even know what to ask first. Or more troublesome is asking questions that are driven from the perspective of the researcher who may be oblivious to or assign vastly different meaning to the culture under study. Beginning with observation and not questions is a good way to avoid overt bias from the beginning.

## Why Participant Observation?

The process of community research depends greatly on the ability of the researcher to build rapport and credibility among the community. Researchers may find themselves under suspicion at first so beginning by asking a lot of questions is not always a good strategy. Participant observation allows the researcher to see and be seen by others. Over time, the researcher becomes something of a fixture in society and much of the suspicion fades. Now, people may be more open to answering the researcher's questions.

As stated above, observing a community or event first can raise questions the researcher wants to answer that he or she may not have thought about ahead of time. Observations lead to questions, and questions may reveal more things that need to be observed. This process will be described in more detail below, but suffice to say that participant observation is the best way to begin work in a new community.

## Levels of Participation

At a basic level, participant observation is living among the people being studied, taking note of all that is happening, and recording data.[1] Living among the people is the best way to see all of life as well as build rapport that will allow people to feel comfortable with the researcher and not hold back. Not everyone is able to live among the research community long-term, however. In other instances, a series of shorter-term visits may be the only available

---

1. Fetterman, *Ethnography*, 34–35.

approach. Either way, the researcher desires to experience all that can be experienced in order to best view the culture through the eyes of its members. A number of legal and ethical concerns are raised as to how fully one is able to participate so a few guidelines should be considered.

## Nonparticipant Observation

There may be instances where the researcher does not want to participate in the activity for legal or ethical reasons, but observing the activity is still helpful for the research process. Several examples come to mind. I have observed many religious acts in various Hindu temples, mosques, and the homes of religious adherents. I do not participate in these rituals alongside the followers. It is best to be clear up front that you will not participate but would like to observe what is going on. I have never been told no in these instances. I will sit in the back of the mosque and take notes or walk through a Hindu temple and look around. I do not want locals to incorrectly think I am an adherent to that religion. I have a friend who was once at a ritual in India that required the killing of a dog. None of the Indians felt comfortable killing the animal and were discussing who should do it. My friend spoke up and said, "I grew up on a farm and we killed lots of animals. I'll do it!" And he did. It may have been clear to the Indians that this guy was helping them do something unpleasant and was not actually participating in the ritual, but I would not have killed the dog because I would be helping others carry out a religion that I felt was wrong. There are likely many situations where Christian researchers would not ethically want to participate, but might still observe.

In other instances, there are legal constraints to participation. It is certainly helpful to understand how gang activity, drug-dealing, and prostitution impact a community. However, for obvious reasons the researcher would not want to participate in drug deals to better learn their dynamics. In some instances the lines become blurred. What should a researcher do if he or she wanted to learn more about why underground church networks are effective, but those networks are illegal in the country? Is it okay for the researcher to attend meetings even though this attendance breaks the law? There is no easy answer for situations like these but I keep a few guidelines in mind. I try to err of the side of safety, both for myself but more so for those I am researching. It is better to have less in-depth information than to get a house church arrested by my mere presence.

Finally, there may be instances where your participation is not culturally appropriate. I have a friend who was researching the Dinka population in Louisville, Kentucky. The Dinka had fled persecution in Sudan and were resettled as refugees in Louisville. My friend had done a great job building relationships with the Dinka and was invited to attend a wedding dowry negotiation ceremony. This was a great honor for my friend and crucial to the research to see how an important cultural practice like a dowry negotiation would be conducted outside of Sudan with none of the normal currencies like cows. However, it was not appropriate for my friend to participate in the negotiation itself. He, and the Dinka, were pleased to allow him to be there and watch what happened. In summary, while nonparticipant observation might sound like an oxymoron, it is still a vital research tool in situations where the researcher should not actively participate for ethical, legal, or cultural reasons.

## Partial Participant Observation

Partial participant observation is likely the most common level at which researchers will work. This level of involvement typically means the researcher joins in with community activities, but the presence of the researcher is not crucial to the success of those events. A good example is joining a family for a meal. The meal would go on with the researcher, but the researcher is able to learn much from time spent at the table. In these instances, the researcher joins whatever activities are happening to the fullest level possible. A few years ago I was part of a team researching the Bengali population in Queens, New York. As we walked the neighborhood we found a cricket game in full swing. Several of our team members joined in the game for about thirty minutes. We learned much about the attempt for these Bengali immigrants to maintain their cultural identity in an immigrant setting. Playing cricket was not just something fun to pass the time, but more deeply, it was a place to really *be* Bengali in the midst of a diverse community.

People in every community go through seemingly mundane daily events, but it is in the midst of these events that community is built. Birthday parties, weddings, meals, family get-togethers, sports, school, work, tea-drinking sessions, and many other events are where real life happens and are the very places researchers need to be. It is best to spend as much time as possible in the community at the widest variety of events in order to get the deepest picture of what is going on, what unites people, what gives them a sense of cultural identity, and so on.

## Full Participant Observation

Full participation means the presence of the researcher is essential and integral to the success of the event. This level of involvement typically only happens when the researcher lives in the community long-term. Examples include serving on school boards, city councils, ethnic advocacy groups, or actually being employed in the community. In these instances, the researcher is not only there to observe, but to be a part of the community identity-forming process. The researcher has a vested interest in the community beyond simply learning more, and he or she has the power to effect real change.

Full participant observation can happen in the workplace. Many churches, ministries, colleges, and businesses do not spend enough time reflecting on their own culture and health. It is a good idea to, from time to time, conduct an insider's assessment of your organization. For example, I once taught at a college with a sizable minority student population. Over time, I began to notice some of these students expressing frustration with "the administration" over a lack of voice and representation. I started paying more attention to the interactions of minority students with majority students, the racial and ethnic makeup of faculty, administration, chapel preachers, musicians, and so on. It did not take long to see that from a minority perspective, no one seemed to care about what they thought and what their experience was like at this school. I saw these feelings expressed in anger among some students. All was not well. A friend of mine had conducted a self-study at his college on the minority student experience and found some troubling, but helpful information. I approached my administration with some of my observations and concerns and asked that we might also conduct a self-study.

I have had many students who have undertaken similar projects at their churches. Sometimes these students are met with a brush off, but other times the leadership takes their ideas seriously. Recently one student visited me to tell me how she had talked with her church staff about evaluating the effectiveness of the church's evangelism efforts. A team was formed and they began to systematically observe from this new perspective what the Sunday service felt like, small groups, outreach events, and so on with an aim to see who attended these events, who did not and why, and whether these events were successful to draw in new believers. Again, the research team had the power to affect change, so they were able to be full participants in the research process.

Each researcher will likely adapt a variety of levels of participation, from non to full depending on the circumstances. Ethical, legal, cultural, and time constraints typically reveal the proper level of engagement. In most instances, the more participation the better, but the goal in all cases is to build relationships, see all that can be seen, and begin to formulate questions to ask regarding the meaning of these events. Now that an overview of the approach to participant observation has been described, I will give detail as to how the process works and what kinds of things to look for.

## How the Process Works

A friend of mine has worked with Hindu Nepali refugees for the past ten years. He has a great relationship with many in the community and lives in a neighborhood where several Nepali families have bought houses. My friend is regularly invited to their homes for meals, tea, and to catch up, and he reciprocates with invitations to his own house. My friend was invited to the wedding of two of the Nepalis he had known for some time. There was a reception and meal after the ceremony. My friend and his family were directed to a small room off the main hall from where all the Nepalis were eating. Finding this placement odd, my friend began trying to inquire why he was seated away from everyone else, especially given his longtime relationship with many in the hall. Answers were not forthcoming. What was going on? Eventually he was able to get a younger Nepali boy to explain. This was a formal, high-level cultural event and my friend was not of the proper caste so he could not eat with everyone else, lest his presence pollute the food.

This story is a great example of how observation can lead to insight into how culture works. The likely reason my friend was excluded from this meal when he had literally eaten with these people in other contexts was a higher level of cultural identity at this formal event, coupled with heightened community pressure to conform to Nepali culture since so many people were there. Was this an insult to my friend? No. Did this placement reveal a double standard and his "friends" had never really cared for him all along? No. It was simply insight into how culture works differently in public and private contexts. Participant observation gives the researcher access to this insight, if he or she only knows what to look for.

## Who Is Present, and Who Is Not?

Typically, the first category I look for when visiting a place for research purposes is demographic. I simply make a note of who is there. What kinds of people are there, are the genders equally represented, how about age groups, skin tones, and so on? How are people dressed; are different people dressed differently?

In many cases, it is equally important to ask not only who *is* there, but who *is not* there and why? Use the same categories as above—what kinds of people are not there? Are there certain ages, genders, skin tones, etc. that are not represented at the event? In some Muslim homes a visiting man will not see any women.

*Participant Observation*

There is a cultural reason for that. Use these observations in all contexts—churches, workplaces, grocery stores, parks, schools, PTO meetings, rallies, etc. and you will gain insight into the local relational dynamics of the community. There may be a good reason why some kinds of people are not present and this information might make all the difference in understanding an area when planting a church.

## What Are People Doing?

Along with observing who is present and who is not, researchers should make note of what people are doing. Again, use the demographic categories above and look around. Who is doing the cooking, who is interacting with whom, what kinds of conversations are happening, who plays the sports, are people touching each other, if so, who and how, etc. These observations will begin to reveal appropriate cultural roles in the community that might need to be considered for ministry strategy. For example, if it is not appropriate for men and women who are not married or related to be in the same room together, it might not be appropriate to have mixed gender exploratory Bible studies as an initial outreach strategy.

Cultural role is especially important in major cultural events like weddings, funerals, religious celebrations, and so on. Find out who the leaders are at these events and who has power and influence in the community. These people may be the gatekeepers who need to give their permission to you as a researcher or missionary in order to live in the area or build proper rapport and relational credibility. Write down something about everyone present if possible because you never know what might be important and you simply haven't realized it yet.

## The Physical Space

Along with people, the space itself may have cultural significance. Take note of how the place is arranged. The neighborhood in which I lived in Malaysia had a mix of quality of housing. Side by side were apartment complexes seemingly falling apart and others that sparkled with care. The rent of these various units ranged dramatically. As a result, the neighborhood was filled with a wide variety of kinds of people. In Malaysia, income level can often be tied to ethnic group, with certain groups tending to be wealthier than other groups. Thus, my neighborhood had a wide variety of ethnic groups in addition to economic status. I didn't give this observation much thought at first, but later began to wonder why this neighborhood was so mixed because oftentimes wealthier people do not want to live next to poor people. My observations led to questions. I found out the government has a policy, or at least a strategy, to unite the diverse peoples of Malaysia under a campaign called One Malaysia. Part of this strategy is to require neighborhoods to have many housing options from low to high in hopes of drawing all the main ethnic groups of the country together. In general, these groups do not get along well so I began to ask around my neighborhood what people thought of this strategy and found great insight into the perspectives of various people and how ethnic groups viewed themselves and others. This insight is crucial for effective ministry.

Physical space can be used to communicate culture. Corner offices have significance, the architecture of places of worship matters, the arrangement of tables and chairs is carefully thought out. Make no assumptions and record the arrangement of everything at first. Again, you may later realize great significance in the physical layout of a city, neighborhood, building, or classroom. Different cultures fill the same objects with different meaning and symbolism so do not assume things are working the same as they might in your house or culture.

## Public Space Is Not Neutral

Physical or public space is not neutral as well. My apartment complex in Malaysia had a nice pool on site. One day I took my kids to the pool and found it empty except for one Muslim lady and her young boy at the very opposite end of the pool. The lady was standing on the steps with water up to her knees holding her son's hand as he played. One hundred feet away I sat on the edge of the pool and put my feet in. The moment my feet entered the water I noticed the Muslim lady get out of the pool. A few minutes later I got out and sat on a chair. Shortly thereafter, the Muslim lady entered the pool again. I was now intrigued. I went back to the pool to see what would happen. Sure enough, the moment my body entered the water the Muslim lady got out. Cultural norms were at play. The public pool is not a neutral space for all to enjoy equally.

I know a church with a conviction to be multiethnic and reach the diverse community where the believers live. The church bought a building in the small downtown area of the city. The building had exposed brick, an industrial warehouse look, and was near the neighborhoods filled with the kinds of people the church wanted to reach but hadn't yet found success. Yet, years later the racial dynamic of the church has not changed. What happened? While the church is not itself in a residential neighborhood, its physical location is not neutral and is not inviting to all. As a white male, I am welcomed as I walk the streets around the church, which are filled with high-end boutiques, law offices, and micropubs. Yet, I am sorry to say that the African Americans who live just outside of downtown would likely not be met with the same welcome as they walked those same blocks. They may be viewed with suspicion.

These are important dynamics to observe. A physical space may be welcoming and inviting to me, but not to someone else. Almost all physical space is governed by cultural dynamics of who is accepted. My church building, with its warehouse look, exposed brick walls, and coffee bar has a distinct cultural feel. I don't say this to be derogatory in any way, but these kinds of churches tend to attract hipster types and my church is no exception. Show up and look around and you will find in abundance tight pants, long beards, and black horn-rimmed glasses. These people are godly and welcoming, but the physical location and look of the space is not to all people. Simply put, the layout and use of physical space greatly matters in many cultural contexts.

Peoples on the Move

## Map the Area

It is a good idea to draw a physical map of the area under research. The scale and complexity of the map depends on the context, whether it be a single room or entire neighborhood. The researcher need not have a degree in architecture; a simple drawing will suffice. Represent the physical configuration of the place and draw in any key physical objects. It's fine if nothing is yet known about these objects; that information can be added later. Maps of neighborhoods may include location of places of worship, ethnic distribution, parks or playgrounds playing a role in the community, gang territories, etc. It may be necessary to draw several maps of different spaces in the area of research.

Maps provide a visual representation of a culture-making space and may reveal how the community uses different areas to unite or divide space related to identity. For example, the apartment complex where I worked with Nepali refugees contained a section on the grounds that was tilled up and could be rented for community garden space. I soon found that many Nepalis spent large amounts of time in the garden working the soil and growing vegetables they used in cooking that they could either not buy at a store or could grow more cheaply themselves. Over time I found that the garden represented more than simply a place to grow food. It was the place where Nepalis could reinforce their ethnic identity. Many of them had been farmers prior to displacement so being able to work the soil again, even in a foreign country, brought something familiar and crucial to who they were. The same complex had a large common room where people could gather to watch TV and find information about jobs and ESL classes posted on the bulletin board. The common room was a fairly neutral space at the apartment. Thus, it was here we decided to host our Bible storying classes that also taught conversational English. Nepalis were already used to using the area and saw the common room as a place to connect with the outside world for English and jobs. It was fascinating to me how these two spaces, the garden and the common room, each played a crucial, but vastly different role in the lived identity of the Nepali refugees.

## Making Sense of the Data

As noted above, observation leads to questions. After spending time at an event, the researcher should have a long list of things about which to ask. At the Nepali community garden I noticed stakes near each plot with variously colored ribbons attached. I assumed these colors marked whatever kind of vegetable grew there. I've learned not to assume and to ask about everything, even for fear of looking completely ignorant. In this case, I found out those ribbons were there to ward off any spirits that may cause harm to the crops. This was an important finding related to the religion of the Nepali in a diaspora context. It is a good idea to observe first, sometimes even for several visits and then review your notes on the physical space and begin asking questions about what you've noticed. At some point, however, the information from your interviews will lead you to investigate new physical areas, or revisit previous ones with fresh eyes. Thus, the research process becomes cyclical. Observations lead to questions and answers lead to more observations.

Avoid doing too much analysis at this early point in the research process. You are still deeply immersed in the learning process and may infer wrongly as to what everything means. The presence of Hindu gods in an apartment complex may not mean the people are deeply religious. Or, as in the case of many lower-caste Nepalis, Hinduism is a veneer thinly laid over a largely animistic worldview. The time for analysis will come later, after a large body of observations, interviews, and notes has been recorded. For now, remember Sherlock Holmes and see everything, even things others do not see when standing in the same room as you. Make note of it all, even if you think things insignificant. Then ask questions, deep questions, as to the meaning of the physical space.

# 8

## Qualitative Interviewing

### Introduction

I WAS SITTING ACROSS from my Nepali friend, a college student, who was struggling with a dating relationship. This was not the typical American story, however. This woman, a higher-caste Hindu with a largely secular worldview, was studying in the United States and had met a boy. He was from a lower-caste, Christian ethnic group in Nepal, and also had a largely secular worldview. These two were of similar age, had similar interests, were both well outside their homeland and its culture, and, to them, religious boundaries and caste restrictions seemed an oppressive yoke of an outdated society. They were in love. The woman's mother had forbidden the relationship. Her reasoning was simple. If her daughter broke caste by marrying this man of lower caste, not only would her daughter pollute herself and ruin her next life, but the daughter would then be unable to perform the proper funeral rituals at her mother's death and would hinder her mother's prospects of reincarnation. That's pressure!

Talking with this Nepali student gave me great insight into changing culture, family relationships, cultural identity outside the homeland, and how religious labels can simply be a veneer masking the true underlying worldview. Observation alone would not have allowed me such insight. On the surface, I would see a young

Hindu woman making her way in the United States. I would see a young man who most would assume was also Hindu. Few would have observed any problems with the relationship. In these settings, qualitative interviewing is a crucial tool for deep culture learning.

## What is Qualitative Interviewing?

### A Window In

Qualitative interviewing, in essence, is simply asking questions to learn. Conversation is a skill that everyone already possesses to some level. Done well, it is much more than a mere conversation, however. It is a window into people's lives and experiences. It helps the researcher see the world through the eyes of the interviewee. Only around 20 percent of culture is visible on the surface. We can observe language, dress, interactions, and religious practice. We cannot, however, observe *why* and *how* these external actions shape identity and worldview. Qualitative interviewing opens the blinds so we might see in. Otherwise, we likely fall victim to false assumptions about people and communities.

Qualitative interviewing is also a way to reconstruct events in which the researcher did not participate.[1] People tell stories of events that shaped their lives and cultural identity. These past events have ongoing implications and it may be essential for the researcher to know something of these events for current ministry. Church members may have had bad experiences with a pastor and are now suspicious and unwilling to quickly follow the new pastor's ideas for change. Without knowledge of these events the pastor may find opposition or even hostility and be the only one who doesn't know why!

---

1. Rubin and Rubin, *Qualitative Interviewing*, 1.

# Peoples on the Move

## A Tool to Develop Meaning

The previous chapter demonstrated the value of participant observation. The researcher should now have a long list of notes about the physical space, people present, people not present, and notes on interactions. Now, qualitative interviewing gives depth and insight into what is going on in those interactions. What meaning is assigned to those objects? Why do those people talk with each other, but not these people? Why am I seated outside the main hall at this Nepali wedding banquet? What is the purpose of that community garden? What is the meaning of that ring on your finger? Why does your wife always walk behind you? There are endless questions that probe for deep-level meaning and interpretation of the visible culture.

Anthropologist Clifford Geertz advanced the idea that material culture is symbolic of underlying worldview.[2] There is no inherent meaning in physical space and physical materials. People supply meaning, or interpret meaning, based on their culture and then assign that meaning to the space or object. There is a precise bodily form that is followed for daily Islamic prayers. Simply performing that physical motion with my body does not somehow automatically make me a Muslim. However, if I were to perform that motion in a room of Muslims, they would interpret my actions to indicate I am a Muslim. In this way, different things and different spaces can function radically differently in various contexts. A Quran sitting on a shelf above the door of a Muslim's house is not simply a convenient place to store the book. Some Muslims follow this practice to keep evil spirits from entering the house and causing harm. The only way to know how physical space is used and interpreted culturally is to ask.

## Community-Based Solutions

Americans are often driven to solve problems. We like to fix things. The quicker something is fixed, the better, so we can move on to

2. Geertz, *Interpretation of Cultures*.

the next problem. Such an approach comes across as brash, rude, and domineering to many cultures, however. Additionally, when we arrive with a "what's wrong and how can we fix it" mentality we tend to overrun the local culture, disempower people, or use culturally inappropriate solutions. Qualitative interviewing allows the researcher to find out from within if the "problem" is really a problem and if it is, what is the most appropriate community-driven manner to solve it?

A friend of mine and her husband are medical missionaries in East Africa. She recently emailed me asking for advice. Many people were dying in the community of easily solved medical issues, at least from a Western perspective. It would be easy for the doctor to simply tell people to stop doing some things, start doing others, and get this or that surgery and much of this needless death and suffering could be eliminated. Her dilemma was that her mission agency trained them to not impose themselves on the culture, not fix things, and not exert their outside, Western influence. Should they only share the gospel, or go on to risk upsetting the local community by making suggestions as outsiders? They had been there a year. Not a long time, but enough time to have made a few friends and gained the respect of many in the community because of their love and service. My suggestion was to consult a local whom they trusted and had a good relationship and raise this issue. Note that as outsiders, this is what they have noticed and they had some ideas how life might be improved, but they did not know the culturally appropriate way forward. Ask this local person what they thought would be best, and if moving forward was it, how could that be done in the most appropriate manner? In this way, the missionaries could learn from a local and let the local person take ownership of the issue and pave the way forward if necessary.

Qualitative interviewing draws from local insight and empowers locals to be the change agents. In many cases, if change is an insider's idea and is implemented by insiders, success is more likely. If the outsider simply dictates "do this or that," they may find resistance, resentment, or create a disempowerment of locals.

Many people are deeply familiar with the issues in their own community and often, the best and most appropriate solutions come from within. You as the researcher have an entire community of experts at hand who have the resources to solve problems. It may be that what you think is a problem is not of concern and would have been a waste of time and money if it was addressed. The only way to know is to ask, but to ask with the posture that the locals are the experts.

## The Role of the Researcher

In many ways, the researcher, or interviewer, is the most important component of the interviewing process. Well-practiced, adaptable researchers can make the most of any situation, but overly nervous, unprepared interviewers can clam up even normally talkative people. Thankfully, like most of the entire community research process, practice can greatly improve the qualitative interviewing process.

## Be Flexible

Interviewing is fascinating to me because I never know what I'll get when I talk with someone. I enjoy hearing people's perspectives. People can be difficult however! Some people will talk incessantly and rather than needing a prompt, they need a halter. It takes skill to know when to let someone talk and when to pry in a redirection. Others hesitate to talk and only give yes and no responses.

Effective interviewers go with the flow in most cases and don't get flustered when encountering the occasional unusual person. Poor interviewers tend to be rigid and try to control the conversation too much. Watch people in news or sports that are great interviewers and learn. The best make the process look easy, so easy, it's easy to underestimate how difficult good interviewing actually is. The good news is there is always someone else to talk with, so if this particular person or interview is going poorly, no need to worry. Just begin anew with the next person. Community research is forgiving in that way.

## Listen First

Good interviewers are great listeners. Qualitative interviews are not debates so there is no need for the interviewer to be "making a case" in their own minds while someone is talking. Focus totally on what the person is saying, how they are saying it, and what they may not be saying. The best information typically comes in the follow-up questions, but the researcher will not know what to ask if he or she hasn't listened first and listened well.

People will reveal what is important in their responses. The researcher does not need to know everything to ask at first. Follow up for more depth based on what the person is talking about and what seems important to them. "Why" and "how" questions follow "what" questions. Good interviewers make people feel like they are the center of the world at that moment. Since much note-taking is often done after the interview, it is extremely important the researcher listen well, follow up well, and listen again.

## Be Relaxed

Nervous interviewers lead to nervous interviewees. Take a few deep breaths and prepare yourself before talking with someone. Have a few key questions in mind to begin the conversation and go from there. The first thirty seconds of a conversation are the most awkward so being prepared and not fumbling the beginning goes a long way to ensuring everyone is at ease. It's easier to at least appear relaxed when listening to someone else talk, so don't talk too much! Usually there is no need to make jokes or break the ice. Just ask the person if you might talk to them for a few minutes about the neighborhood and their experiences. If people do not want to talk, move on to someone else rather than forcing a conversation. Be ready to give people an out if they begin to feel uncomfortable during the interview. Let them know ahead of time they are free to break off the interview at any point. Again, there is always someone else to talk to, so any one person is not overwhelmingly important.

Practice goes a long way for improving interview skills and remaining relaxed. I created an activity that has worked well. I create a series of short interviews in training. I ask the group to come up with a category, which can be anything at all—the more interesting the better. Then I ask for a volunteer to come and interview me. They get thirty seconds to formulate their initial questions related to the topic. I then set a five-minute timer and the person interviews me. I try to be a good interviewee and answer their questions well. I let awkward pauses remain. The five minutes actually goes faster than most people think. After the timer goes off, I ask the person how they think they did, what they did well, and what they would change for the next time. Then I ask the group what they learned about me during the interview and what other follow-up questions they might have asked. I continually encourage them to look for questions that draw out deep meaning and perspective rather than just factual questions. People love this activity. It helps them get to know me, practice their skills as interviewers directly, but also indirectly as they listen to others interview, and do so in a safe environment.

## The Interviewee

In qualitative interviewing, the interviewees are the gold mines of information. As noted above, some people are more talkative than others and some are better at providing the right kind of information than others. Everyone can be coached and at the end of the day most people end up knowing more than they think they might. A few tips can help the process along.

## Qualitative Interviewing

### A Partner in the Research

People in the community are partners in, and not objects of, the research. Some people feel they are not the ones to talk with and that they do not know enough to be helpful. Good interviewers help people to see differently. These local people live in the community. They are the experts. They have the perspective. Their views and experiences matter. Encourage people to share from their experience and not their "knowledge" if they are hesitant to talk.

It may be that people view you the researcher as the expert and continually defer to you. In these cases I remind people that I'm an outsider and I would love to hear what they have to say. Even in places where I have lived longer term I still tell people a story or two about how I am always learning more from local people and so enjoy hearing about their experiences. Usually, these brief examples of how I've learned from others helps people to be more at ease and more likely to talk with me.

### An Individual

Even though communities produce culture, every community is made up of individuals with their own take on life. Good community research requires thorough interviewing. It is not enough to interview a person or two and feel a good sense of the neighborhood dynamics has been realized. People have individual experiences, feelings, opinions, and perceptions. It is important to interview a wide enough variety of people to have as accurate a representation of the entire community as possible. Even very homogenous communities have some variance in people's experience. Treat every person as a new person who should speak for themselves and let them fill in the blanks to the questions.

The best approach is to actively engage a wide variety of people. Interview kids, young adults, middle age, and the oldest people in the community. Interview both men and women. Married people and single people may have different experiences. Find people of varying levels of education and work experience.

Interview people of different ethnic and racial makeup. Make note of how long people have lived in the community and try to talk with some newcomers and some lifelong residents. It's often the experience of newcomers that neighborhoods are not very welcoming, though lifetime residents may feel the opposite. The researcher never knows what kinds of people may have experiences key to understanding the area or formulating a more effective ministry strategy.

Good interviewing can take a lot of time. It likely requires several visits, even for the shortest of research projects. If time allows, the goal is to interview until a point of saturation is reached. Not everyone has to be talked to, but after you begin to hear the same kinds of responses from a variety of people, you know you are getting close to having surveyed enough people for an accurate representation of the area. Formal research projects for academic purposes should make use of sample size calculators that can be found online. These calculators will tell the researcher how many people need to be surveyed based on the overall population in order to have a statistically accurate sample size.

## The Interviewing Process

### Finding People to Interview

The first step in interviewing is finding people with whom to speak. Walking the streets and looking for people in public is a good start, but what of those you do not see? There may be a reason certain kinds of people are in public and others are not. Again, a wide variety of kinds of people is best. Talk to shop owners, residents, people at bus stops, community centers, libraries, the police, and in places of worship. Some of these people likely work in the community but live elsewhere. They may have a different, but important, perspective than residents.

I make a point of finishing every interview by asking the person if they know anyone they think essential to whom I should speak. It is even better if they can introduce me to that person and extend their credibility. I've used this approach to find informal community leaders who opened doors to research that I never could have known about. Someone told my team that we needed to speak with the Iqaluit elders in Nunavut. They said they met Tuesday afternoons at a certain place and that we needed to bring a specific meat tray from the grocery store as currency to be invited in. Who would have thought that's what it would take to stand before the elders? We did so and the interviews with the real leaders of the community were a wealth of information.

It is important to not make assumptions when looking for people with whom to talk. I try to continually come across as a learner and impress on every person that they are the expert I have been looking for. One student used this approach and later realized she was talking with the American ambassador to that country and hadn't realized. The ambassador was so impressed with the student's approach that she invited the student to meet other ambassadors and to help as much as possible with the research project. That's the beauty of community research—you never know what might happen!

## Conducting the Interview

The first thing to consider when conducting interviews is the ethical obligation you have to protect those with whom you are speaking. It is important to decide ahead of time if there will be limits to what you do with what you hear. It is standard procedure to offer people anonymity and the opportunity to stop the interview at any time. Let them know what you plan to do with the information. People may share something that could get them in trouble with their family, coworkers, neighbors, or even the law. Have a plan to assure people the information they divulge will not be used against them. If you have a limit to the confidentiality you can provide, state it up front. For example, you might say that everything will be kept confidential unless they tell you about a crime that has happened or that they know is likely to be committed.

Formal research projects, especially those that are federally funded or done for academic programs require prior approval from an ethics committee that often wants to know the purpose and procedures for the research and see the interview questions ahead of time to gauge risk for those under study. More informal or ministry-based community research does not require these approvals, but it is still important to keep ethical guidelines in place to protect those you are working with. It is not necessary that everyone sign an informed consent form before you interview them for most projects. However, do not push too hard for information or use manipulation to get more detail than someone is willing to give. If taking notes raises too much suspicion, don't take notes. There are always more people to interview so it is not necessary or helpful to push any one interview too far. Additionally, do not make any promises you cannot keep, such as what great changes will come to the neighborhood as a result of your study.

I usually begin by introducing myself and asking the person if it's ok if I ask them a few questions about the community. How I introduce myself depends on the situation. I tend to be more open about what I'm doing unless I find it raises unnecessary suspicion. I might say I'm with a local church, school, or live in the area and am trying to learn more about the neighborhood. People do not always have a category for "researcher," so I avoid that title. If I find that my introductions are not working well, I will try a different approach with the next person.

Qualitative interviewing is fairly open-ended by nature. Researchers do not arrive with a long list of predetermined questions. I may begin by asking a little about the person's background, how long they have lived in the area, what they do, etc. Then I ask whatever questions are relevant to my study. Interviews often follow whatever is important in that particular conversation. I may refer to something other people have said and then ask this new person their opinion. It takes skill but you can learn to read a person and press for detail when you feel there might be more the person knows. The main point for qualitative interviewing is rich detail beyond the surface-level response. Why do people feel the way they do? Can they give an example of that? What events have they experienced that led to those feelings? How are their perceptions impacting how they relate to others? My research often centers around issues related to culture, race, ethnicity, religious belief, and relational dynamics in the community at the intersection of these topics. I usually want to know how people perceive one another, why they interact with some but not others, and what drives these views. Such information is useful for me to formulate a ministry strategy taking into account these dynamics.

I always conclude the interview by thanking the person and then asking if they know anyone else I should talk with and if they can introduce me to that person. I will address note-taking later, but in general, I do not take notes while conducting the interview but stop somewhere immediately after and record my thoughts before moving on to talk with someone else. I will certainly forget important details if I continue interviewing others before writing my notes.

I am in favor of researching in small teams. Depending on the context it may be helpful to have a mixed-gender or mixed-ethnic team. Sometimes it is better for a nonwhite person to talk to a nonwhite person because they may feel more comfortable with the perceived power dynamics of the conversation. I have had Asian interviewers tell me that other Asians felt they were better understood by a fellow Asian and were more inclined to talk. In other instances, it may be better for a white interviewer to interview a nonwhite interviewee. Try a variety of combinations and see how it goes and adjust accordingly.

## Recording the Interview

Interviewers must decide ahead of time how to keep track of information gathered during the interviews. The most sure way to not miss anything is to film the interview to capture both audio but also body language. Few people feel comfortable being filmed, however. Even the presence of an audio recorder can intimidate some people. It is not ethical to secretly record people so if you plan to use a recording device, tell people up front and get their permission. I rarely record the interview unless I'm doing some kind of linguistic research or a formal interview. Most of my interviews are done on the streets or in various shops or homes.

I focus on the person as much as possible and casually conduct the interview, trusting I will remember what is helpful, but not worrying about trying to remember everything. As soon as the interview concludes I get out a small notebook and begin writing. I write as many details as I can remember—who the person was, any demographic information about them, and then key words, themes, quotations, and as much detail about the interview as possible. I do not know at that moment what will be important so I write as much as I can and sort that out later.

I typically do not carry a computer or tablet because I don't want to get robbed. A small notebook with a waterproof cover works best. In the past I have sometimes used a research app on my phone. These apps are always changing but I primarily used one called FieldNotes. I could mark the location on a GPS, take pictures, record videos, write notes, or record audio notes and sync it to that particular interview. The data could later be exported and sorted by theme, keyword, etc. and even loaded into a GIS mapping program where the data pins would populate the map. I could sort the pins by any demographic marker I wanted. Try different note-taking techniques until you find what works best for you in your situation.

At the end of each day's research I sit down in front of a computer and retype my notes, assign an identifying letter or number to the interview, add anything else that comes to mind, and write any follow-up questions or places I need to visit based on what I found that day. It is tempting to begin to analyze the data each day and form conclusions about what is going on, but it is best to wait until a larger body of interviews have been completed before any analysis is done. Too early an analysis may seat false or incomplete ideas in your mind that begin to color how you approach other interviews.

## Conclusion

Qualitative interviewing is at the heart of good community research. It focuses on the people themselves, their perspectives, experiences, and roles. Interviewing often follows participant observation but leads to knowledge of new places and events to visit. The process can be intimidating but every researcher can gain interviewing skills and over time the work becomes more natural, more comfortable, and often one of the most enjoyable aspects of community research. Several days, weeks, or months of observations and interviews leaves a mountain of data. It is to the analysis of this data that we now turn.

# 9

# Data Analysis

## The General Process

AT THIS POINT IN the research process, there will likely be a large amount of scattered data. The researcher has pages and pages of notes from participant observations and interviews across a large time span, geographical area, and demographic range. The researcher probably has many thoughts about the culture of the area, how people interact, and what is important. It is difficult not to form a solidified conclusion, but a key point in ethnographic research is to let the themes rise from the data themselves.

Data analysis must occur so that the research drives the conclusions and the conclusions are clearly supported by the research. In a way, the process is similar to studying Scripture. For those who believe in authorial intent, it is inappropriate to conduct a cursory scan of a passage and then come to your own conclusions. A detailed examination must take place, looking at grammatical structures, surrounding biblical and cultural context, and flow of the passage. In this way, biblical meaning rises from the text and the text clearly supports the conclusions of the study.

Intuitive researchers may be able to arrive at a fair conclusion as to what is going on in the community, but bias may creep in and the researcher may subtly arrive at preconceived conclusions. Readers and others benefiting from the community research process want to be sure they can trust the findings and the most sure way to demonstrate that trust is to carefully analyze the data and then draw conclusions.

Data analysis can be an intimidating and confusing step in the research process, but like many other components, it can be broken down into a process. I will provide a brief summary here and then explain each step in detail below. The first step is to read through all the notes, observations, and data several times to seat the material in the mind of the analyst. Eventually, the scattered notes will begin to form a coherent narrative describing the community. This initial readthrough lays the beginnings of that structural foundation. Next, the researcher must find some way to categorize or group the data into manageable segments. Perhaps data is drawn together relating to family structures, language use, religious practices, and interaction with others. Alternatively, the data might be grouped according to a history of the neighborhood, then the demographics, and then the culture. There are many ways to categorize the data so choose one that is best suited to the purpose of the study. Finally, the researcher looks for key themes that emerge from the categories of data. What is most important to the people? What factors bound their identity? These themes are essentially the explanations for how the community operates and how people relate to themselves and to others. It is from these themes that appropriate ministry strategies are later developed.

## Making Sense of the Initial Findings

My team was nearing the end of a week's worth of intensive research in London, England. Part of our group had focused on an open-air type market where vendors could rent stalls and sell their fruits, vegetables, and other wares. We had been told the market was locally known as the Latino market because it was dominated by Latin American immigrants. Technically, the market was known as the Seven Sisters Market because of the area in which it was located. As we interviewed stall workers we began to realize the area was an important place for not only Latin American food and goods, but for Latin American identity. Here, these immigrants could be themselves, speak their language, play their music, and find their foods. Over and over we heard stories and quotes related to these cultural markers. Latinos could feel secure in their own identity in the face of a very diverse London.

Then we came across an Asian immigrant who had a stall in the market. In our interview with her, we referred to the place as the Latino Market and asked how she became connected with the area. In response, she strongly stated, "This is *not* the Latino Market. This is the Seven Sisters Market!" Whoa! What is going on here? Clearly, we had touched a nerve with this lady and her response alerted us to something important with which we needed to take note. We followed up with several questions probing her response and experience in London and this market.

In short, as an Asian, this woman did not feel welcome even though this was a market dominated by other immigrants. The area had taken on a Latino feel and culture which did not extend to her as an Asian. Since much public space is not neutral, the geographic area had much more symbolic meaning than simply a general immigrant market. As I mentioned above, it became a place where Latinos could reinforce their cultural identity, thus to them, this was the Latino Market. The very markers of Latino identity that united that group served to exclude this Asian. In her effort to carve out a place where she belonged she was adamant this was the Seven Sisters Market. Calling it by its formal name allowed her, in her mind at least, to belong. She felt like she didn't belong if it was the Latino Market.

We did not fully arrive at this conclusion in the midst of the interview itself, but we made note that her perspective was an important one, and one that was different than the general responses we had been getting in our interviews. When a researcher arrives at the analysis stage, there will be an overwhelming amount of data that cannot all be used as is in the final write-up. The difficulty then is what to use and how to make sense of it? I include this story because as we poured over the hundreds of pages of notes from our week of research, we highlighted interviews like this one with the

*Data Analysis*

Asian woman that seemed especially significant in understanding the overall culture of the place.

Data analysis is a series of steps or comb-throughs that gradually whittle and condense an immense body of potential findings. Researchers must find some way to represent their data in a usable and meaningful way. The initial readthroughs help make sense of the broad scope of data and are used to mark segments that seem especially good at representing the bigger picture and which will be followed up in the later stages of data analysis.

## Categorizing and Grouping Data

The next step in the analysis process is to sift through the data yet again and assign related groups of information to corresponding categories. This process is technically called coding, but essentially involves grouping and categorizing. There are two broad approaches to the categorizing process. The first is to come to the data without preconceived categories and see what arises and then assign the data to groups. The second is to have a general framework of categories and then assign corresponding data to those categories.

### Data-Driven Categorizing

Let's say I am undertaking a study on minority student experiences at a local Christian university. I have recently finished a series of observations and interviews with African-American students, Hispanic students, international students, and Third Culture Kids. My initial readthroughs indicate that different groups of students seem to experience the university differently but I begin to see patterns of responses. Again and again I see the word "representation" in the interview notes. It seems some students do not find others like themselves in official positions and capacities around the school. Few faculty are people of color. Chapel music rarely reflects their cultural style. Retreats and campus ministry events seem to focus on camping, shooting guns, and riding horses—something urban dwellers find unappealing. In short, some minority students do not feel welcome and accepted on campus.

I later begin to notice a series of comments from international students about life in the dorms. There is not access to any means to cook food and the standard cafeteria fare seems to be making them sick. Worse is the policy to close the dorms over long breaks such as winter break and spring break. Students can stay in the dorms but have to pay an additional fee. Worse still is the cafeteria being completely closed during these breaks. International students mention not having a car and other American students have gone home, leaving the internationals to subsist on loaves of bread or Ramen noodles for an entire week or more.

Data-driven categorizing draws together these comments, perspectives, and experiences and creates categories to represent these ideas. From the example above, I may create groups related to dorm life, religious events on campus, and experiences in the classroom. Together, these groups paint a larger picture of a general theme among minority students—their experiences are not understood by the majority group, including faculty and administration, and lack of understanding leads to feelings of under representation, anxiety, and sometimes perceived hostility.

The difficulty with data-driven categorization and analysis is to avoid imposing the researcher's ideas onto the data. Categories form as common words, experiences, perceptions, and concepts emerge from the data. Anyone should be able to look at the categories of analysis and clearly see a connection to supporting data in the notes and observations. Each study produces its own categories for analysis, as the data reveals what is important to the interviewees and what themes create a narrative of their experiences.

## Framework-Driven Categorization

The framework approach to categorization is one I often use in my own research. I have developed a general worldview identification tool based on five categories: family, friends, food, festivals, and

## Data Analysis

the future.[1] I create sub-questions in each category tied to whatever culture in which I am working. This approach helps me ask categorically similar questions in my interviews so when it comes time to analyze the data, I comb through my notes and pull out quotes, stories, and experiences and paste the data in a new document under its appropriate category.

This system works well for me on smaller projects and produces a consistent kind of write-up that is useful for church planters and missionaries. Strategies for engagement, relationship-building, and contextualization are driven by the findings in each of these five cultural categories. The next chapter addresses writing up and presenting the findings of community research and often the broad structure of my write-up follows the Five F's approach.

Each researcher may create a set of predetermined categories in which data can be grouped and analyzed. The Five F's works well when researching people groups and communities but would not be appropriate for a study on minority student experiences or some aspect of institutional culture such as research conducted on a church. The goal is to create categories that cover a broad sweep of general components of the culture under study and then fill them out with findings from observations and interviews.

The danger of the framework approach is the possibility to overlook important categories that the researcher may not have been aware of prior to the study and analysis. The key is to look for data related to a new category emergent from the research that is outside the preconceived groups. One or more new categories will likely emerge. The framework approach may allow for quicker grouping and analysis and is appropriate for nonacademic studies.

## Emergence of Themes

The final step in the data analysis process is discovering major themes that are at work in the community. The previous categorization process can be likened to making bricks. The loose data are

---

1. I first encountered the Five F's from my friend Bryan Galloway and have adapted it to my own needs. See Appendix 1 for a model of the Five F's tool.

the raw materials that are gathered, categorized, and baked into a cohesive brick. Big-picture themes then are similar to the building that is built from those individual bricks. Only now does the overall scope take shape.

Themes often center around broad, seemingly vague concepts such as identity, shared culture, belonging, defiance, community, and worldview. They are the essence of what it means to be a "people" in the community.[2] How do people experience their "neighborhood" and their "community" differently? How do minority students experience the university as a culture group? What does it mean to "be Hmong" in a central Wisconsin diaspora setting? What is a Great Commission culture in a church context? What brings a cohesive small-town identity that repels outsiders? Each of these broadly sweeping questions is answered with categorical segments that build the puzzle. Each categorical segment is built from representative data from participant observations, qualitative interviews, and other research conducted previously in the community. There should be a clear and obvious pathway from the raw data to the emergence of themes that explain the unique dynamics of the community.

Someone unrelated to the research team should be able to read through the themes and be able to make sense of the community. If my church-planting strategy has been unsuccessful I should be able to read the results of the research and say, "Oh! Now I know *why.*" As a teacher or professor who has struggled to connect with minority students, I should now be able to understand the difficulties from the students' perspective and hopefully move from frustration and judgment to compassion.

Themes reveal what is important to people, what gives them a sense of meaning and belonging, and what happiness is. Different people in the same community may answer these questions differently and these nuances are crucial for a healthy and effective ministry strategy. Themes arise from within microcommunities and the researcher then analyzes across these themes to understand macro-themes as well.

2. Rubin and Rubin, *Qualitative Interviewing*, 252.

*Data Analysis*

## Preparing Themes for the Final Write-up

Data analysis reveals themes explaining the community but must be fit together in a way that can be written up to both answer the initial research question and also enable understanding by the readers who may not have been part of the research process.[3] Final write-ups may be centered around a handful of the most prominent and comprehensive themes from the research.

A key theme may be identity. The data reveals that people in this particular community understand identity through several smaller themes like language use, ethnic makeup, religious expression, and food. This particular city does not have a concentrated geographic area with large numbers of people from that group. Yet, research reveals a shared sense of belonging through a collective cultural consciousness that is not tied to geographic location. People live in multiethnic neighborhoods, but have their finger on the thread of "their people" that winds through a seemingly incoherent ball of yarn forming the geographic community. Research reveals a number of places that serve as cultural intensifiers where they can be themselves and get recharged so to speak. This group feels a sense of neighborhood pride because of its welcome to them as immigrants, but their real sense of identity is found in their relation to their people across the entire city.

This kind of analysis is crucial for church planters who are deciding which strategy is best. Should they plant a multiethnic church because the neighborhood is so diverse? If so, what language(s) should be used, what style(s) of music, and what food(s) at fellowships? Are there particular peoples who do not get along so it would be unreasonable to expect them to attend an English club together? Perhaps the themes of identity reveal that it is best to plant a mono-ethnic, monolingual church in order to reach pockets of immigrants with a very high level of ethnic and linguistic identity. Where should the church be located? How is public space viewed and used? What initial strategy is needed to draw and connect with unbelieving people from that community?

3. Rubin and Rubin, *Qualitative Interviewing*, 254.

These are the kinds of questions that should be spurred in the minds of both the researcher and the reader when analyzing and writing up key themes found in the community. Thus, in the write-up, the researcher should write with this audience and these important questions in mind. Effective presentation of themes should trigger many "ah ha" moments in the minds of readers and will get them thinking about appropriate strategies that may work based on the themes found in the research. Again, researchers cannot write all the data or the report would never end. Preparation of themes for the final write-up reduces the data to a manageable set of major themes that best represent and explain the community. Rubin and Rubin summarize the process in a helpful way as they write, "the data analysis ends when you have found overarching themes and put them in the context of the broader theory [explanation of the community] and answered the question 'So what?' Then you write the final report."[4]

---

4. Rubin and Rubin, *Qualitative Interviewing*, 256.

## 10

## Writing Up and Applying the Research

### Introduction

THE FINAL STEP IN the research process is organizing the data and deciding on the best way to present and use the findings. This chapter addresses those two aspects, which are intertwined. I first describe the process of writing up the findings and then move to the application of the data. However, it would also be appropriate to address application first since the structure of the write-up necessarily includes a section on application.

### Writing Up the Data

Data and findings are not usable or accessible to anyone but the researcher if the hard work of organizing and presenting the findings is not done. The fruit of such an extensive project can be multiplied by making the findings broadly available as appropriate. The ethnography can be used as a training tool for church members and mission teams who are interested in joining the work. God may use the work in other ways as well. My write-up from Iqaluit, Canada had a long section describing the amazing revitalization of the language and culture of the Inuit in the face of Anglicization. Later, I was at a conference addressing the needs of missionary work in the

Amazon basin in South America. A leader from New Tribes Mission (now Ethnos360) was talking to me about the decline of indigenous languages in the jungles. I shared with him some of the findings as to how the Inuit had successfully addressed these issues and the man asked that I send him the ethnography and maybe they could apply it to language revitalization in the Amazon!

Additionally, the write-up can be used as a mobilization tool to recruit additional workers. For example, I posted on the internet the write-up from the Inuit project and about two years later I received an email from a guy who had found the ethnography. Reading it led to a journey of God calling him to move to Iqaluit and plant the first evangelical church in the area. I shared the write-up from my work in the most diverse zip code in Louisville, Kentucky with a new pastor who had recently been called to a church in the area. The church was in need of revitalization because over the years the demographics of the neighborhood had changed but the church had not and consequently it slowly died. This pastor was overjoyed to receive a detailed write-up of the people groups around the church and a strategy to begin engagement. None of these things would have happened if we had not taken the time to write up our research findings in a useful way.

## Consider the Audience

The first thing to consider is who is the intended audience of the write-up? It may be pastors, church planters, missionaries, missiologists, or other academicians. This book is primarily targeted toward pastors, church planters, and missionaries so I will not address formal academic writing here. Nonacademics do not need literature reviews or extensive interaction with social science theories within which to seat the research. In my view, the best writing is clear writing because clear writing is the most accessible to readers. Most practitioners want a general overview of the findings, themes, and explanations of community dynamics and then a move toward application.

Several presentation styles may be considered. It is possible to summarize the findings in a podcast style production lasting thirty to sixty minutes. Other ideas include a video narrative where the researchers incorporate footage from the community, interviews with residents, and analysis by the researchers. The most common means of presenting findings is typically in a written report of some kind. These need not be dry and filled with endless footnotes. When well-written and well-structured, they are interesting, accessible, and helpful.

## Structuring the Write-up

I typically use a written report to present my findings, but other means of presentation can follow the structure of a written document. There are many ways the data can be structured, but I tend to follow a general pattern that includes four or five major sections. I begin with an overview of the project as a whole. Where is it located, why is the research necessary, and what methods were used to conduct the research? I may describe the team if one was used. This section is typically only a page or two in length unless the write-up is for a more academic audience.

Next, I give an overview of the history of the community. When and how was it founded and how has it generally changed over time? Were there recent migrations, annexations, gentrification, school mergers, or other events that have a lasting impact on the current community? If the research is for a local church or mission team, I may include a brief history of those entities and how they came to be where they are today. In short, include anything helpful in providing an understanding of how current dynamics came to be. Current realities do not come to be in a vacuum. This information is gathered from library research, government websites, and interviews with longtime residents.

The third section presents the current demographics of the community. What people groups are present, roughly how many people compose these various groups, what kinds of work do people tend to do, do they live in homes, apartments, or some other dwelling? What religions are represented? What churches are active in the area? This data is gathered from national and local censuses, city databases, chambers of commerce, local libraries, and interviews with community residents. Local immigrant communities often provide a different, and perhaps more accurate, accounting of their numbers and locations than do government databases. It is helpful to present both. Research done on institutions may provide a different set of demographic categories. Choose whatever is helpful for the research project and audience.

Fourth is a section on the culture or essence of the community. This section is the heart of the ethnography and is typically the longest and most detailed. Here the writer presents the findings of the interviews and observations, major themes, and an overview and explanation of what is going on in the community. There are a number of ways to organize the culture section. Options include a structure driven by the major themes arisen from the data analysis step. These big-picture themes can be arranged in a coherent fashion and used to describe the culture. Another option is to use the Five F's mentioned in the preceding chapter to structure the culture section. Simply subtitle the section with family, friends, food, festivals, and future and fill out each category with the findings derived from data analysis.

The last section I typically include in a nonacademic write-up is the application of the findings to ministry. I detail this process more below, but it entails making recommendations for ministry strategy driven by the findings and themes from the research. This is the "so what" section of the write-up. It may be additionally appropriate, especially in academic writing, to include a further section on areas for future research that this particular project was not able to address.

In short, a thoughtful structure to the write-up organizes the material, helps with connections between ideas and sections, and moves the reader along at a pace that makes the material accessible and impactful. Good writing is clear writing. The use of headings and subheadings is helpful to provide a visual breakup of the pages and allows a reader to quickly locate a particular section of interest.

*Writing Up and Applying the Research*

## Writing Style

Ethnographic writing carries its own style. It "requires an eye for detail, an ability to express that detail in its proper context, and the language skills to weave small details and bits of meaning into a textured fabric."[1] Ethnographies should be interesting to read, full of stories, quotes, and insights into people's lives and experiences. Rich descriptions of places and events draw in the reader as if they were there. Ethnographies may even tug at the emotions of the reader, compelling action.

Another feature of ethnographic writing is called the ethnographic presence. In this discipline, researchers play an active and personal role in the research process. They are in the field talking to people and influencing people and situations along the way. Of course, the goal is not to impose one's self and skew data, but as human beings interact, there will be influence. This phenomenon is acceptable in ethnographic research. Consequently, it is normal and expected to find the researcher(s) present in the write-up. The presence should not appear in a "I went here, and I did this, and then I did that" narrative fashion. Yet, it is appropriate to describe the role of the researcher at events and in conversations.[2] Thus, personal pronouns such as "I," "we," "me," and "us" are allowed. The presence of the researcher in the write-up can add credibility as well. If you feel as if your presence may have skewed the interview, caused someone to be untruthful, or do something they may not normally do, simply say so. I had a student who was conducting research in Malaysia. She was interviewing a man who, after about ten minutes of talking, began to ask the student for her phone number and if she would be interested in a date. Clearly, at this point the presence of the researcher affected data collection so it was appropriate to include this story in the findings.

---

1. Fetterman, *Ethnography*, 111.
2. Fetterman, *Ethnography*, 125.

Peoples on the Move

## Representation and Citation

It is important to clearly connect findings, themes, and ideas to the data gathered from interviews, observations, and other research. Much ethnographic writing seeks to represent the views, experiences, and perspectives of those living in the community. The inclusion of quotes and life stories provides the rich detail that allows readers to feel as if they were there. Ethical issues arise, however, when the stories of real individuals could endanger them or spur repercussions because of what they said. Chapter 8 discusses ethical issues and interviewing, including the need to provide people anonymity when the data is used publicly. The most common way to provide representation with anonymity is to utilize pseudonyms or assign numbers or letters to individuals.

Pseudonyms allow for a more personal experience as readers work through the write-up. They are helpful if several people appear consistently throughout the ethnography and their role is vital to understanding themes and the big picture of the community. It is important to note the use of pseudonyms, typically in a footnote appearing the first time the name is used in the write-up. I have heard on rare occasions, however, of real people being hassled because they happened to share the name of the pseudonymous character in the story and lived in the same neighborhood. In some cases, writers give even the neighborhood itself a pseudonym. Consider this kind of additional protection if writing on areas that are especially sensitive such as missionary efforts in closed or restricted-access countries.

A safer, yet less personal, way to represent people in the write-up is to assign them letters or numbers. Rather than a name, Interviewee 16 appears throughout. Their stories and perspectives still inform and drive the ethnography, but they are better assured anonymity. Be careful to limit the amount of obvious personal description that could be used to discover the real identity of a person. A student of mine was writing on a local YMCA assessing the impact of the after-school kids program. A problem arose when the kids began complaining about the program director.

Their insight was crucial to understanding the dynamic of the program, but how to represent that when there is one clear and obvious director? Assigning "Director T" would not provide any anonymity in this instance!

Another way to allow for real personal experience yet anonymity is to create a fictional composite character based on the experiences of several individuals. This person may be a representation of the typical experiences of someone in the neighborhood. The downside is this person does not exist and no one person shares everything this character is made to experience. Yet, this method does allow for real insight into what it is like to live in the area. The writer must be careful not to write too much personal bias into this character, thus losing credibility with the reader.

## Applying the Findings

The goal of most of the research projects on which I've worked was to produce something that helped church planters and missionaries better understand community dynamics so they could formulate an effective strategy for engagement. This approach is known as applied ethnography. As noted previously, research findings drive the application and there should be a clear and obvious connection between the research and the strategy suggested in the application section. Yet, church planters and missionaries do not work in the vacuum of the community alone. They are not free to employ any strategy that "works." The missionary enterprise rests on both a theological foundation and a cultural application.

### Biblical Foundation for Strategy

Several key questions must be answered from Scripture before any strategy is implemented. The first is what is a biblical church? In my experience, many people seek to reproduce the kind of church they have seen in their own contexts. However, every church is clothed in cultural attire, from the language used to preach, to the style of instrument, to the expected clothing of attenders, to even the physical layout of the space. There is no once for all biblical command for these features of the gathered church. At the foundation, what then is required? Some markers found in Scripture include biblically qualified pastor/elders and deacons, teaching from the Bible, prayer, giving, biblical baptism and communion, intentional identification and gathering, evangelism, and church accountability and discipline.

There are obvious theological disagreements over the purpose and nature of baptism such as whether it is reserved for professing believers only or not. Other issues might include church governance and pastoral leadership. Church planters, missionaries, and other church leadership should have come to reasonable conclusions based on Scripture as to what they deem to be a biblical church. I suggest formulating a document that supports a biblically healthy church, which is not the same as just crossing the threshold from not a church to a church. Scripture does not suggest planting the bare minimum, but contains a host of commands and examples of what healthy churches look like. There is no single passage that contains the full New Testament teaching on the local church. Acts 2:42–47 is a beautiful picture of what was happening in the early church, but does not contain information on pastors and deacons. The church adjusted as it grew in the world and later God-breathed Scripture was revealed to fill out the full scope of what a New Testament church is. Simply put, there needs to be agreement on the essentials from Scripture regarding the nature of the church before people attempt to plant one.

Similarly, the core message of the gospel and essentials of evangelism must be determined from Scripture and not the culture. The means of conducting evangelism should be contextualized, but the content always centers on the life, death, and resurrection of Jesus in the New Testament (1 Cor 15). People must understand the crucifixion in all its redemptive emphasis and respond in repentance and faith in order to be restored to a holy God.

Another point of emphasis is to determine biblically what is the mission of the church. Churches do many good and biblical things such as caring for the poor, stewarding creation, and working in local government for change and justice. The biblical mission of the church certainly includes these things but goes beyond them. The overarching storyline of Scripture centers on the redemptive plan of God to gather to himself a redeemed people from every tribe, tongue, nation, and language. The church makes disciples ultimately—dedicated and growing followers of Jesus, seeking to obey all that he commanded. It is easy to do many good things in the name of Jesus but fall short of making disciples. Once there is consensus scripturally on these and other essentials, church planters and missionaries are now free to learn from their community research and formulate a plan to move forward and accomplish all to which the Bible calls them.

## Relationship-Building

Rapport and credibility are essential for the research process and these same features are essential for effective ministry. The beauty of community research is many of the relationships are already built and remain as the ministry progresses. My research among a Nepali refugee community revealed a need for resume and interviewing workshops and job skills training. These refugees had been resettled and were expected to find jobs to support their families. Our research revealed a number of cultural issues that hindered a collective, indirect communication-based culture interviewing in an individualistic, direct communication American work culture.

We arranged a workshop on a Saturday and invited in the local community and set up stations where we could help refugees translate their experiences surviving twenty years in a camp to a resume to secure jobs in the United States. We printed a stack of twenty resumes on thick, resume-quality paper and proudly handed them to the refugees. Many people, much to our dismay, thanked us profusely and promptly rolled up the papers into a tube and stuck it in their coat pocket! If you think about it, it is rather silly that the thickness of a piece of paper reflects my ability to perform a job! We then moved to a time of coaching refugees to feel comfortable answering questions about themselves, pitching their work skills, and proving why they should be hired. This entire approach was contrary to Nepali culture but the refugees were so thankful to be coached in a safe environment.

Not only did these workshops help refugees with real issues but they allowed a greater degree of trust as we ministered in the community. We learned much about how to communicate with and care for this group. They were family-oriented, had generational gaps in English ability, and spanned a spectrum of religious identity. Our time spent conducting the research was applied to both real life helps and also ministry with these themes in mind.

There are as many examples as there are communities to research. The idea is to learn from the research and use the findings to better connect with and care for the community. Another team I worked with discovered a great desire in the community to work soil and grow vegetables common to the culture so several people pitched in and built a number of raised beds that served as a community garden. This garden then became a place to connect with refugees. These are examples of community-driven solutions to problems and challenges. Too many times, outsiders think they know what is best or what people need and fail to ask the people themselves. Community research allows locals to have a voice in and ownership of their community and its development which produces a stronger, more self-sustaining neighborhood.

## Church Planting

The ultimate goal for most of the research projects on which I've worked was to plant healthy, disciple-making churches. The application of research is essential for how this process works. Research reveals what language is best for ministry. With the Nepalis, we learned that the younger generation wanted to learn and use English, the older did not, some knew how to read a Nepali script, others could not. The situation was complicated further because none of those ministering knew Nepali. Based on our research, we used the following approach: We used a Bible storyset that was written in two columns, Nepali on the left and English on the right. We passed this out when we gathered. A native English speaker read the story in English, then we played an audio recording of a native Nepali speaker telling the story. We asked someone in the group to repeat the story in Nepali, and then in English if they desired. We then split up into discussion groups where we practiced conversational English based on the story. We handed out audio memory sticks with the story in Nepali so they could listen again at home. This situation was not ideal, but based on what we found to be the needs in the community, it was the best approach.

Research can reveal the best place to gather for church as well. I was part of a church-planting team reaching international students at a large public university. Many of these students, including a number of Muslims, did not feel comfortable attending an American church in a traditional building. Many did not have cars and it was too time-consuming to pick people up each week. We ended up gathering with the church in various apartments on or near the campus. Internationals were already used to meeting in each other's apartments for food and fellowship, so it was not intimidating for them to meet and explore the Bible in the same environment. An additional key was we were able to model the simplest form of a church as we could in hopes it could be reproduced when these students went back to their home countries, many in places hostile to the gospel.

A final piece of application is to discover key worldview issues that must be addressed in ministry. Many of the Nepalis with whom I worked would identify as Hindu. However, these were low-caste Hindus who were more animistic than anything. It would not have been appropriate to address Hindu gods or the general Hindu worldview since these were folk Hindus at best. They had an entirely different set of struggles than a higher-caste Hindu might have. There was another group of Nepali refugees in the same city who were high-caste Brahmins. Their Hindu identity was much stronger than the Nepalis with whom I worked. Before we knew these dynamics, a network of churches had brought in a Nepali pastor from Nepal to attend a local Bible school as well as work with the refugees. The first thing that happened was the high caste refugees refused to talk to this man, or even ride in a car with him. The pastor's caste had cut him off from ministering to half the refugee population. To the Americans, these were all Nepali refugees that essentially seemed the same. But this was not how the Nepalis themselves understood their identity. In the end, our discoveries in research radically shifted our strategy for ministry.

## Conclusion

The goal of community research is ultimately to build the kingdom of God. Without a write-up and research-driven application, the fruit of the research is limited to the research team itself. Many pastors, church planters, and missionaries are not academics and do not often undertake extensive writing projects, but the effort spent on these ethnographies multiplies itself for many years. A delivery format matched with the needs of the church planters makes the findings accessible. A suggested strategy based on the findings saves time and provides a strong foundation on which to begin ministry. As noted, these write-ups are useful for training and mobilization and consequently, carry the fruit of the research far beyond the research team.

## 11

# Special Considerations for Multicultural Research and Ministry

## Introduction

MULTICULTURAL SETTINGS POSE UNIQUE challenges for research and ministry. As such, it is appropriate to devote a chapter to the social structures of these societies. Many church planters are interested in planting multiethnic churches, and for good reason. However, these churches are difficult and often, in my experience, unsuccessful. A diverse neighborhood does not automatically result in a diverse church even when one is planted at the intersection of a variety of peoples. Social and ethnic identity is oftentimes more important than geographic proximity. Unless one clearly understands the formation and expression of ethnic identity, multiethnic churches will almost certainly struggle.

At least three key factors must be accounted for in order to understand ethnic identity:

1. ethnicity is essentially a social boundary that shapes attitudes and actions toward others,

2. ethnic distinction plays out in a number of social and cultural differences between groups that form the boundary and allow one group to be able to say "they are not like us," and

3. assimilation is a form of change that occurs as people determine how to live out their identities in the midst of a new culture.

As assimilation occurs, individual ethnic origins become less relevant as individuals on both sides see themselves as more alike than different. This definition of assimilation allows for the influence of the mainstream culture on the immigrant group but also allows for movement by the mainstream toward cultural values of the immigrant group. Ethnic distinctives do not have to disappear, yet assimilation is still possible.

## Forms of Capital

Immigrants face many choices as they adapt to life in the United States. Strategies are formed, usually with the second, third, or even future generations in mind. First-generation immigrants ask what will be best in the long term? Generally, two main strategies are possible, depending on what skills and background the immigrant has. First, there is the "ethnic" strategy which relies on the social network of the immigrant. Second, there is the "mainstream" strategy where the immigrant attempts to enroll children in the American educational system, learn English, and enter the mainstream economy. These two assimilation strategies are often dependent on a theory known as forms of capital. Those following the mainstream strategy typically possess what is known as human capital while the ethnic strategy is driven by what is known as social capital.

## Human Capital

Human capital refers to a person's high level of education and work experience, traits they possess within themselves. These immigrants tend to be professionals and live in the middle class or above in their home countries. They have college degrees at the least and many have masters or doctorates as well. They tend to migrate in families,

## Special Considerations for Multicultural Research and Ministry

seeking a more permanent settlement in their country of destination and desire to reestablish their middle- and upper-class lifestyle. Often, they live in the suburbs of major cities. They bring money and skills that allow them to assimilate into mainstream American culture, if they choose. They avoid ethnic enclaves because they want their children to have the best education, learn English well, and successfully enter the mainstream economy.

Asian immigrants tend to compose the majority of those immigrating with high levels of human capital. Two subgroups include Filipinos and South Asian Indians. These groups come from countries where English is widely spoken and education opportunities are numerous. These two immigrants groups bring a professional class of doctors, educators, and technology specialists. These groups usually raise children that excel in school, earn professional and graduate degrees, and often marry outside their ethnic group.

### Social Capital

Social capital is the counterpart to human capital. Those possessing social capital are primarily labor migrants. They lack education and technical skills—human capital. However, they are in touch with a vast network of social relationships that span the gap from their small home villages to larger gateway cities where they leave their home country and continue to their destination in the United States. These immigrants rely on word-of-mouth as to the right time to migrate, how to navigate a border crossing, how to find that first job, and how to get by in the States. Such a reliance on social networks produces a dependence on those who have gone before them. These workers are more likely to be exploited, earn low wages, and have little opportunity for advancement. They are not as likely to stay long term in the United States as those coming with high levels of human capital.

Social capital migrants primarily come from Mexico and other Central American countries, the Caribbean basin, and a smaller stream from China. It generally takes longer for these immigrants and their children to assimilate and join the mainstream economy.

If the second generation only attains a high school diploma, their education has already far exceeded that of their parents. Dropout rates in school are high. These immigrants navigate life in a different way than those with human capital. In summary, the forms of capital theory helps one to understand and predict patterns of assimilation of peoples from around the world. The assimilation models stemming from the forms of capital theory will be explained in more depth below.

## Assimilation Models

In broad strokes, assimilation takes on three major forms. First, ethnic enclaves form when an ethnic group is bound in a dense geographic location. Enclaves often contain the least amount of assimilation, at least with regards to the ethnic group moving toward the mainstream culture. Second, some immigrants do not group geographically in an enclave, but they form tight social networks among themselves that function like cultural threads linking them together over a dispersed geographic area. Third, the urban tribe mentality requires the most amount of assimilation as individuals from multiple groups drop aspects of their culture and form a distinct, new cultural identity. This new group is composed of highly heterogeneous individuals living as a group in the mainstream urban culture or sub-culture of the city.

### Ethnic Enclaves

Ethnic enclaves may be the most prominent image that comes to mind when most Americans think of immigrant groups. In general terms, an enclave can be any form of immigrant concentration within a loose geographic boundary.[1] However, true enclaves rely on further connections than simply spatial. Technically, enclaves contain immigrant groups which concentrate in a distinct spatial location *and* organize a variety of economic enterprises serving

1. Guest and Kwong, "Ethnic Enclaves and Cultural Diversity," 291.

their own ethnic market and/or the general population.[2] This definition is both geographic and economic.

The nature of enclave economies often leads to exploitation of workers. Kwong found that the Fuzhounese enclaves in New York's Lower Manhattan and Brooklyn Chinatowns were controlled by a mafia-style system. In this case, Chinese smugglers have set up human importation businesses and bring illegal Chinese to the United States. In return, the immigrants must pay a $50,000 transportation debt and remain at the mercy of business owners, much like an indentured servant, for years. Compliance is enforced via threats, torture, rape, and kidnapping. Additionally, immigrants are made to work long hours and are paid well below minimum wage. Kwong concludes that this enclave provides an easy entrance into America but seriously questions the long-term benefit of such a system.[3] Assimilation is low because new arrivals do not need English and rely on their ethnic community for all their needs. It is not likely that enclave residents will leave their neighborhoods or attend multiethnic churches.

As a whole, ethnic enclaves are dwindling in the United States. They rely on a continuous stream of first-generation immigrants who lack the human capital necessary to survive without the enclave. Little Saigon, a once prosperous Vietnamese enclave in Orange County, California is declining as the second and third generations are assimilating into the mainstream culture and moving out of the enclave. They now have the human capital of English, education, and skills to support themselves. The most dramatic changes occurred over a five-year period in the 1990s as more than 800 businesses closed in the enclave.[4]

In summary, ethnic enclaves are those neighborhoods composed of a high-density population of a singular or small number of ethnic groups. These enclaves contain economies run by and

---

2. Portes, "Modes of Structural Incorporation and Present Theories of Immigration," 291.

3. Kwong, *New Chinatown*.

4. Do, *Vietnamese Americans*. See chapters 4 and 5 for an overview and assessment of the Little Saigon enclave.

for fellow members of the group. The enclave environment is not a cultural utopia in the midst of the city, but carries its own problems and characteristics.

## Cultural Threads

A second model of assimilation is what I call the cultural thread model. Immigrants with a high degree of human capital, such as Indians, often place job consideration over the tendency to settle in an enclave environment. For most people, community is rooted in a sense of place, but these immigrants often build a collective cultural consciousness. They share a cultural identity that leads to the idea of community, even though they may live miles apart from each other. The concept can be defined as "recent populations of shared ethnic identity which enter an area from distant sources, then quickly adopt a dispersed pattern of residential location, all the while managing to remain cohesive through a variety of means."[5] Immigrants first prefer to seek out informal networks where they can feel connected, determine their social status in the new environment, and begin their new life. Later, they find or create more formal organizations that serve as a cultural unifier and reinforcer for their ethnic group.

The organizational means that link the ethnic group together in community may be churches, temples, mosques, community centers, business associations, bars, ethnic grocery stores, ethnic malls, ESL centers, annual cultural festivals, and so on. For example, the ethnic community in Dallas–Fort Worth lacks the enclave phenomenon. Groups have created this shared sense of ethnic consciousness, however. Indian, Chinese, and Korean groups have bought old shopping centers and converted them into ethnic malls, each with a large grocery store that caters to their peoples' food. The malls contain restaurants, clothing stores, and travel agencies.

These centers of cultural exchange provide a place for migrant community affirming events. In US urban centers, these events reinforce the cultural identity of the ethnic group in the

---

5. Zelinsky and Lee, "Heterolocalism," 281.

face of segregated everyday life which pulls the individual into mainstream American culture. In the case of an Indian immigrant, attending a festival helps the person feel more "Indian" and affirm his place as an Indian in American society.

An additional "place" that needs to be taken into account is the virtual realm. Ethnic groups often produce websites, chatrooms, and discussion boards where they can connect, stay abreast of the latest news from their home country, and provide advice for incoming immigrants on where to live and work. One example is the Ek Nazar website and database for the Indian community in Dallas and other cities.[6] The website contains not only information but is an economic entity as well. Travel agencies use the site to market to Indians traveling back home for vacation or for a permanent move.

Interestingly, the general population is often not aware that there is any connection between their Indian neighbor and the thousands of other Indians in the city. Church planters can mistakenly assume that immigrants in a diverse environment lose their individual ethnic identity and take on general characteristics of a multicultural neighborhood. Such was the thinking of missionaries in London who were using a general church-planting strategy and English language when attempting to reach neighborhoods with diverse ethnic populations. Ethnographic research revealed that the majority of immigrants there were connected via this cultural thread and had much less in common with other ethnic groups than could be found on the surface.

In summary, the cultural thread model of assimilation consists of creating community through establishing habitual places of contact, congregation, worship, and ethnic identity confirmation and reinforcement. Groups most likely to assimilate via this model are those with high levels of human capital that have no need to group in an enclave environment. They may live dispersed throughout the city but remain connected through their social thread.

---

6. See http://www.eknazar.com/.

# Peoples on the Move

## Urban Tribe

The urban tribe model requires the highest amount of assimilation to the local culture and context. In some ways, it is a model of its own rather than at one end of a scale of level of assimilation. The concept arises because diversity is one of the markers of an urban area. As such, in urban settings, people groups cannot be studied in isolation. Culture is increasingly marked by hybridity.

In some instances, city life encourages the formation of subcultural groups that function like a tribe within the city.[7] Individuals from diverse backgrounds share a common affinity that transcends their ethnic and cultural identity. These new communities may be based on ethnic or linguistic affinity, while others are based on shared interest in sports, business, school, and a host of other markers. The urban tribe concept rejects the idea of individualism as it is widely conceived in the West. Cities appear at first to be an undefined mass and a faceless crowd. However, there may be cohesion in that crowd that is unnoticed to the casual observer. There is a "tribalism consisting of a patchwork of small local entities."[8] These entities are made of a shared identification that becomes the basis for community. People in urban centers may desire to identify with others, and the process in itself creates a diverse union of seemingly unalike people.

Urban specialist Ethan Watters concludes that urbanites may share much in common and even form bonds as strong or stronger than their biological family ties.[9] Chris Clayman, a church planter working with immigrant groups in New York City, writes:

> Migration reshapes people group boundaries. Even in their home countries this takes place with urbanization, and many immigrants to NYC came from urban areas that are not considered "their ethnic homeland." So, we have many immigrants here that have been through, or are going through, two or more urban filtering processes

---

7. Fischer, *Urban Experience*.
8. Maffesoli, *Time of the Tribes*, 9.
9. Watters, *Urban Tribes*, 3, 7, 19, 49, and 58.

in regards to their ethnic identity. Many of these [people] start having a much broader sense of their people group identity and a result.[10]

Clayman appears to be describing a scenario where people are moving "up" a level in their cultural identity. For example, in Nigeria a Yoruba tribesman sees himself as distinct and very different from a Housa, though they live in proximity to each other in the same country. To an outsider, they may even appear to be the same people. After immigrating to a city like New York, however, the two peoples may drop their identity as Yoruba and Housa and simply think of themselves as Nigerians or even West Africans.

The implications of this thinking and the urban tribe concept in general inform the level of specificity and contextualization a church planting strategy needs to have for reaching people groups in an urban diaspora context. Does one need to learn Yoruba or will English suffice? Can a Yoruba and a Housa—traditional enemies—be expected to attend the same English class together or even a Bible study together in New York City?

The urban tribe theory may have its limits, however. Watters describes a group of individuals who, on the surface, seem very different. However, they are much more alike than he alludes to. In his study, all are recent college grads, are at similar life stages, and share many common interests. They likely all share a general worldview. They do not come from diverse religious and cultural backgrounds like people groups do. Their distinctions are much more social than ethnic, religious, or cultural. A common worldview is the bond and allows for ease of interaction at the social level. My theory is that the urban tribe concept breaks down at the worldview level, not the social level, and people groups bring different worldviews with them, thus any apparent urban tribe type interaction might be only surface level.

Surface-level cultural accommodation is often a means for survival for new immigrants. Depending on the background, some first-generation immigrants develop the skills necessary to

---

10. From Troy Bush, personal email with Chris Clayman.

survive but rarely procure more than entry-level jobs. They may suffer what Hiebert calls status shock as they are unable to do the work for which they were trained in their home country.[11] My own ethnographic research on Nepali immigrants in Louisville confers with Hiebert. I interviewed immigrants who had been doctors, screen printers, and mechanics prior to their years in a refugee camp. Now in the United States, these immigrants did not have the English skills or the culturally appropriate credentials to find similar work in Louisville. As a means of survival, Nepali, Iraqi, and Caribbean immigrants would come together for classes to learn English, study for the citizenship test, or learn to drive but once their immediate personal benefit ran out, they did not associate with each other. My research in London produced similar findings. Immigrants from a host of Latin American countries and a handful of other people groups would gather together for English club. On the surface, they seemed to be an urban tribe, sharing a common affinity despite ethnic differences. They lived together in apartments and sometimes traveled together around the city. Once missionaries attempted to use the English club as a launching point for a Bible study, the "tribe" suddenly disappeared. That diverse people lived together could be explained as a result of the visa and housing problems immigrants dealt with in London. It was very difficult for an immigrant to live where he wanted. Often, he had to take the first opening he could find, regardless of the geographic location or current ethnic makeup of the housemates.

Alba and Nee write that those of similar ethnic origin tend to have higher levels of trust and intimacy with each other. As people assimilate into mainstream culture, they tend to extend their trust and intimacy in an increasingly broad circle, past their own people group.[12] However, first-generation immigrants rarely, if ever, fully assimilate into mainstream culture. Many immigrants will undergo selective acculturation. Immigrants drop their own cultural identity and acculturate just enough to survive but the

11. Hiebert and Meneses, *Incarnational Ministry*, 285.
12. Alba and Nee, *Remaking the American Mainstream*, 260.

## Special Considerations for Multicultural Research and Ministry

acculturation is very superficial.[13] This surface-level accommodation does not impede on core worldview beliefs. I believe that in some cases, particularly with international college students who are very Westernized, the urban tribe theory holds up. However, strategies for church planting should not be developed on the assumption that all diaspora populations in general will adhere to the theory. Field research is essential to determine the level of acculturation and assess if the appearance of an urban tribe mentality goes beyond surface level.

In conclusion, it is true that immigrants from diverse backgrounds do interact with each other to some degree. Hiebert writes that "we must see the city, therefore, not as a homogeneous place, but as hundreds of subcultural groups living and interacting with one another in the same geographic area."[14] However, each subgroup has its own cultural distinctions. Sometimes, people will gather together based on a shared affinity for English, a profession, or a social interest. The validity of the urban tribe is still in question and church planters should research the unique dynamics of their own neighborhoods before making too many assumptions.

### Formation of Cultural Identity

Hall writes that instead of thinking of cultural identity as an already-accomplished fact, it is better to think of identity as a production and process that is never finished.[15] This understanding is especially important in the diaspora and immigrant context where pressures of the multicultural nature of urban life constantly challenge understandings of identity and belonging. In the diaspora, Hall believes immigrants form a culture of multiple micro-identities in the midst of the larger mainstream culture. This sense of culture carries the idea of both becoming and being as the immigrant struggles to reconcile past, present, and future understandings of

---

13. Gibson, *Accommodation without Assimilation*, 1988.
14. Hiebert and Meneses, *Incarnational Ministry*, 271.
15. Hall, "Cultural Identity and Diaspora," 234.

cultural identity.[16] Families have a shared past but are adjusting and assimilating to a new culture in a new geographic location. A child asks his father, "Am I Indian or American?" and is given the answer that he is both.[17]

## Cycle of Cultural Identity

The path of immigration, choices made regarding level of assimilation, and then an understanding and expression of cultural identity is a difficult process. Identity is not static but moves along a spectrum, and moves at different paces for different people. A common scenario plays out with four steps on the path to assimilation and cultural identity. First, the immigrant leaves the home country because of all that is wrong there—the political corruption, poverty, the war, etc. Second, the immigrant embraces the new country for all of its idealism. The myth of the American Dream draws people willingly to the United States more than any country in the world. Third, life does not go as the immigrant desires. He becomes disillusioned with the United States and begins to look back at the good of the old ways from the home country. Fourth, the immigrant must decide to either live a balance of the old identity coupled with the new, abandon the old ways, or embrace and intensify the old ways but now in an idealized way.[18] The challenge for church planting is determining where people are on this spectrum and if their views are changing.

The dominant culture of the United States plays a role in immigrant identity as well. In essence, racial and ethnic prejudice can force minority groups to gather together and intensify their ethnic identity. Blacks become "more black" in order to distance themselves from white mainstream America. A friend of mine, an African American, struggled with his identity in our largely white church. One day he told me he determined to be "the blackest black

---

16. Hall, "Cultural Identity and Diaspora," 236.
17. Radhakrishnan, "Ethnicity in an Age of Diaspora," 119.
18. Radhakrishnan, "Ethnicity in an Age of Diaspora," 125–26.

man in this church." Such a statement is very telling. Depending on where the immigrant and his immediate community are on the scale of assimilation, ethnic identity may be very strong, to the point of rejecting identification as an American who happens to be ethnically Indian.

Radhakrishnan observes three general stages in an immigrant's understanding of ethnic identity. First, in order to be successful in the U.S., immigrants are sometimes forced to hide their distinct ethnic identity and assimilate. Second, after immigrants become more secure financially and socially, they look for a reaffirmation of their ethnic identity. This stage is described above in the section on cultural threads where immigrants assert their right to be different. Third, immigrants adopt a "hyphenated integration of ethnic identity with [U.S.] national identity."[19] These immigrants, by their very assimilation and citizenship in the U.S., are forced to make a decision: Are they Indian-Americans or are they Americans who happen to be Indian? The former retains a bit of ethnic pride and identity. The latter relegates ethnicity to secondary status behind new-found American nationality.

## Public-Private Identities

Often, dynamics of identity vary in public and private life as well. No one in a society can live totally as they wish. Publicly, immigrants often must play the role assigned to them by their employer and follow general cultural norms or risk constant friction. Privately, people can be themselves. This behavior is similar to what linguists describe as code switching, the concept where individuals will speak one language or dialect in some instances but shift to another language or dialect when it is more appropriate given the social setting. Immigrant identity requires a type of cultural code switching that occurs between public and private life.

Because of multiple ways immigrants express themselves, it is vital to know them both publicly and privately. Publicly, it may

---

19. Radhakrishnan, "Ethnicity in an Age of Diaspora," 121.

appear as if they are assimilated into American culture. A multi-ethnic church-planting strategy may seem appropriate. Privately, however, the immigrant may be a different person, reverting exclusively to their heart language, religious worldview, and culture. I have encountered several Hindus who identify as Christians publicly, but have never changed at the worldview level. Being a "Christian" publicly is socially acceptable where they live and affords them benefit. One would never know what is going on under the surface unless a deep relationship is formed and the person is known publicly and privately.

## Conclusion

This chapter, likely the most technical of the book, is helpful in understanding social dynamics in urban settings. Urban ministry brings its own challenges and rewards. The theories presented here on immigrant identity, assimilation strategy, and social networking provide a basis for the kinds of things to look for when conducting community research in the city. These findings play a direct role in decisions surrounding multi- or mono-ethnic church, ministry language, and evangelism strategies. In large urban areas, the most effective strategy is often multiple strategies!

## 12

# Short-Term, Team-Based Ethnographic Research

### Introduction

MANY CHURCHES, COLLEGE AND seminary classes, and missionaries have the opportunity to undertake short-term trips for the purpose of community research. As a missiologist, I have been involved with several of these short-term ethnographic research projects. These special research trips pose a unique setting to carry out the work that warrants special consideration. I have found that a short-term, team-based approach to ethnographic research can be a helpful, time-efficient means of understanding a culture, or a segment of a culture. Most of this book has focused on longer time spans, but compare the two approaches—one researcher can spend two months in an area and put in about 400 hours of research. A team of eight can spend less than a week in an area and put in the same number of total research hours.

I define "short-term" as anywhere from one day to perhaps up to two weeks. One must be realistic about the amount and depth of research that can be performed in a limited time, but with proper planning, training, and a laser focus on the specifics of the research, a surprising amount of good data can be gathered in a few days in the field. These approaches are typically useful for churches, church planters, or missionaries who want to better understand their communities or a new target community for the purposes of developing a strategy for effective ministry and have the luxury of a short term team or mission trip with which to work.

## Two Approaches to Team-Based Research

Here, I give a brief overview of two approaches to the team-based research method that I have used in different contexts, along with pros and cons of each. Later, I will provide an in-depth example of the categorical model in action in Iqaluit, Nunavut and the geographical model used in Louisville, Kentucky.

### Team-Based Categorical Model

In this model, each member of a team is tasked with focusing on a specific cultural category or domain to research during the trip. For example, one member may focus all her research on the linguistic aspects of the people. Another may research the family structures. Yet another will tackle religion and myth in the culture. The team should be formed according to each individual's strength or background with the assigned category. Perhaps someone was a communication major in college and another studied business. Often, I am surprised at the depth of experience and interest team members have, though many had not thought of how their interest would be helpful for community research.

Each person has a specific focus and as the days progress, the research/informant base builds. The most helpful research is often done several days into the trip as the researcher has had a few days to build a general knowledge of the people and has been introduced to knowledgeable informants in the area. Each researcher also has an ear and eye open to informants with knowledge in other cultural categories. Nightly team debriefing sessions afford opportunity to share contacts with other members of the research team. For example, I might be researching linguistics but come across a local business owner. I ask the owner for contact information that I can share with my teammate who is researching the local economy.

### Pros

That each member of the team only has to focus on one cultural category means the category can be intensively researched without distraction. It is surprising how much information can be found on one topic in a few days' time. Furthermore, team members can share contacts so members save time by not having to always set out with a blank slate. College students, seminary or graduate students, and church members typically have some background through school or job that is useful for field research. Assigning each researcher to their area of expertise or interest can make the research more interesting, but also more efficient, as the researcher has prior knowledge of the domain. Finally, the ethnographic write-up comes together more seamlessly because each team member has only to write up their one cultural category. Each small paper can be combined to form the more comprehensive ethnography.

### Cons

The major concern is that each team member has the ability to understand and ask the right questions related to their topic of inquiry. If all members do not have formal research training, several team training sessions prior to the research trip can help. The categorical model can feel isolated as well, as each team member is only responsible for their area of research. The categorical model has limitations in that it is best suited to researching a specific people group or population. In a rural or monocultural setting, this model is idea. However, things are more complicated in a city or multicultural environment. The research focus may be Punjabis in London. This group may be spread over vast geographical distance and it can be difficult for the research team to remain focused only on the research population at hand.

# Peoples on the Move

## Team-Based Geographical Model

This model works better in an urban setting. Here, the research field is bounded geographically by streets, zip code, or neighborhood. My team used the geographical model on the project in London to research immigration dynamics. We split our larger team into groups of two or three. We had four groups total, and each was assigned a borough in London where local missionaries were at work. In this model, each team or individual returns to the same geographic location every day. The geographic model allows a large area to be covered in a short time, providing a general picture of the city to those requesting the research.

In my case, each small team was tasked with locating as many different people groups living in the borough as possible. London was experiencing vast numbers of immigrants from EU-connected countries as well as the Muslim world. We were to find out basic information about each people group such as immigration history, motivation for migration, religion, community leaders, and businesses owned by those from that people group. We were able to discover a basic understanding of the cultural dynamics in each borough, use of space and power by dominant and minority groups, and weave together a larger understanding of immigration, identity, and community in London by comparing research from the four boroughs.

### *Pros*

In a large city like London, the geographic model can provide a basic overview of the city. Specific information about each sub-geographic area helps one understand local and neighborhood dynamics as well as determine if certain themes are prominent in the city as a whole or are confined to certain people groups or neighborhoods. Urban ministry can be overwhelming and this research model breaks the complexity into smaller, manageable segments that can lead to applied context-specific ministry strategies.

## Cons

This model does not allow for the depth of research that would the category-specific model. There simply is not enough time to dig deeply into each people group. Additionally, the final write-up can be somewhat difficult to compile by the lead researcher. The task can be made easier by requiring the same format to be used by each team when doing their write-up. For example, should each team's write-up be categorized by neighborhood within the borough, listing people groups found locally? Or should the write-up be categorized by people group, and then list the geographic locations they reside in under the group? The answer depends on what the one requesting the research is using the research for. Advanced planning is necessary for the write-up to be helpful and organized.

## The Categorical Model in Iqaluit, Nunavut

This section walks through the application of the category-based model used to research dynamics in Iqaluit, Nunavut, Canada. The North American Mission Board of the SBC was considering sending a church-planting team to Iqaluit and contracted my research team to provide an overview of the dynamics of the town. I worked at The Southern Baptist Theological Seminary in Louisville, Kentucky at the time and we put this concept into practice with a short-term team sent out by the school to conduct ethnographic research. The goal was to identify the culture(s), religions(s), dominant language, leadership structures, family relations, and ethnic tensions in the small capital city of Nunavut. The team consisted of graduate students from various disciplines as well as two members of NAMB hoping to do church planting in Iqaluit. The students had completed coursework for an ethnographic research class and the trip was part of the fieldwork requirement.

## Methodology

The team arrived in Iqaluit with no contacts, little idea of how the city was laid out, no previous experience in this part of the world, and five days to learn what we could of the culture in order to gather the needed data for the ethnography. The goal was to find information concerning key research areas: government structure, history, family structures, the decision-making process, effects of racism and ethnocentrism, preference for native language and religion, and to build meaningful relationships with locals to help pave the way for an incoming church planting team.

Upon arrival the team assigned research goals for the week to each member. The team of nine was split into groups of two or three and each group was asked to choose one of the aforementioned research areas. Team members chose focus areas that had developed out of individual interest fueled by various points of training and from their own experience. Assigning research areas to each team member made the overall project manageable in a short amount of time.

## Gathering the Research

The team approach allows different personalities, giftings, and skills to be maximized in order to accomplish the task more efficiently. Some on the team were adept at sitting in a library for hours looking at photographs and reading records. Others were skilled in social settings and had a knack for getting information from informal conversation. The first trip into the city catered to each team member's strength. With no names to seek out or known places to visit, each group simply walked about the town and looked for people with whom they could talk. When one research pair found themselves warming up in a local coffee shop, they discovered that the casual coffee stop proved to be a goldmine for information and networking. It so happened that the city mayor's husband owned the shop. Local government leaders frequented the coffee shop for conversation—both casual and business. Since these particular

## Short-Term, Team-Based Ethnographic Research

team members were conversant in areas of business and politics, they were able to immediately join in the conversation and even contribute to the topics being discussed. The diversity of the team facilitated this effective research and insight into government and politics in Iqaluit.

Other team members spent time in the local museums, bookstores, and the visitor's center. The patient inquirer was able to record valuable information about the history of the city, local industry and tourism, and begin to understand the complex mythology that undergirds the religious expression found among the Inuit. Learning some of the names of local spirits enabled the team to use them in conversation on the street to ascertain the level of animism and spirit worship still prevalent after more than one hundred years of Anglican Church presence.

It was crucial that each team member take accurate notes of any findings. In order to be respectful of the conversation, the notes were usually recorded immediately after saying goodbye. Often, one conversation would provide several leads for further inquiry, as researchers would always ask their informant who else they might talk with and if they might be introduced to that person. In this way what began as a blank slate quickly blossomed into a web of connections around the city. Each team member made a note when the interviewee mentioned matters that dealt with another team member's area of research responsibility. In order to stay on task, this new information was held until the nightly debriefing and was then shared with the other team members.

### Daily Debriefing

Though the Arctic sun never actually set, each "evening" the team met for a time of sharing and debriefing. This proved to be the most encouraging and important time of the day. Every group shared their findings for the day in their particular research category. It was amazing how much information could be discovered, how many relationships were built, and the number of follow-up contacts made considering the short time spent in town. As previously noted, many team members were able to gather information about other member's research areas and discover names and contact information of people they should talk to the next day. The nightly debriefing was a time to confirm findings, encourage one another, and develop a plan for the next day in order to make the most of the short trip.

## Summary

The team's basic strategy proved to be successful. Division of research topics was crucial so that some member of the team covered all essential areas, thus allowing research hours to be multiplied and work done effectively. Relationships and contacts quickly spider-webbed from one day to the next with the evening debriefing providing a time to compile data and share contacts with other team members. In many aspects the trip was similar to what one would find in the United States—quality lodging, recognizable food, predominant use of English, and a town built around the government buildings in the center of town. Upon further investigation however, the team discovered a society consisting of complex layers of culture fighting to coexist. Over the course of the week one could begin to see how much of the culture was built on a foundation of age-old stories that provided the rules of life, explained creation, put forth rituals and methods to appease the spirits, and compile stories meant to keep children safe in the unforgiving arctic climate.

## The Geographical Model in Louisville, Kentucky

I led a class conducting a one-day research project in the most diverse zip code within Louisville, Kentucky. A pastor had recently begun leading a church in the area toward revitalization and wanted help understanding the dynamics of the neighborhood around the church. This project took place during the height of refugee resettlement under President Obama. Since the neighborhood was so diverse culturally and religiously, the geographical model was better suited than the categorical model.

## Methodology

In designing the research project, I bound the target area geographically by using streets roughly a half mile in each direction from the church. Doing so limited the area the team needed to cover, which is essential for quality research when using the geographical model. There were twenty-five students in the class so I divided them into groups of five. I then subdivided the research target area into five sections and assigned a group to each. I attempted to place a mixture of personalities as well as ethnic background in each group in order to utilize a variety of giftings on each research team.

We met for briefing and training in participant observation and qualitative interviewing the day before the research was to take place. After training, I put a Google map of the neighborhood on the screen and pointed out a number of things that teams would use to begin their research. In a geographical model, it is helpful to locate initial points of contact such as grocery stores, libraries, ethnic shops, places of worship, police stations, etc. ahead of time. These areas may prove to hold a wealth of information about local community population and dynamics. I had printed maps for each team marked with these locations.

The goal for the geographical model is to find out as much as possible about that particular area: what people groups are present, where do people live, what work do people do, what is the history of the neighborhood, what major events have shaped the personality of the neighborhood, how do people get along, etc.? The team discovers this information via observations, interviews, and any archival research that may be accessible.

# Peoples on the Move

## Gathering the Research

The team had eight hours to literally walk the streets, visit stores and shops, places of worship, restaurants, groceries, etc. and gather information. We used a research app called "Field Notes." This app allows the researcher to record notes, take pictures, record audio and videos, and drop a GPS locator for each entry. Later, the data was be loaded into a GIS program and sorted in a number of ways helpful for research, such as where Muslims live, people interested in Bible studies, etc.

Each informant was asked who else would be good to talk with and, bit by bit, a fairly extensive network of local relationships, informal community leaders, and layout of the neighborhood was discovered. Asking someone to physically introduce the team to another contact was crucial to build rapport. As with the categorical model in Iqaluit, the research team was amazed at the level of detail they were able to gather in just one day's time. Having a diverse research team was helpful, as in some instances it was better to have an Asian-American student speak with Asian immigrants, or an African-American student speak with African-American community members. Surprisingly, in other instances it was more helpful to have a white student interview an Asian immigrant. The point is a mixed team overall is typically ideal.

## Debriefing

The team met to share research, stories, and thoughts at the end of the day. I uploaded all the GIS data into the program. Each team worked together to find a way to compile their field notes and produce a write-up for their particular geographical area of research. We had an hour or so to process the day and make any further notes that were, in this case, geared toward the goal of the research, which was to provide this church with a picture of its neighborhood and recommendations for strategic engagement.

In the week after, I worked on compiling each team's write-up into something useful for the church. As noted above, compiling the write-up for a geographic model is more difficult than for the categorical model. I divided the paper into five sections for the five neighborhoods and then further subdivided each section into demographics, history, people groups, key leaders, and suggestions for strategic engagement that were grounded in the research.

## Summary

The geographic model worked well in this instance because we were researching a very diverse section of Louisville. The church had asked for a snapshot of the area and were not necessarily looking to engage just one particular linguistic or religious group. It was crucial ahead of time to divide the area into manageable segments that a team could reasonably cover in one day. Sufficient training ahead of time helped ensure the research would be efficient and as accurate as could be expected given the circumstances.

## Assessment of the Short-Term, Team-Based Research Method

In both instances, the research process worked as anticipated. For short-term projects, the team needs to clearly understand the trip objective, the limited time, and the value that this research data can afford. The team process enables a more comprehensive snapshot of culture in such a short time. While an individual researcher can certainly drill down much deeper over a longer period of time, a team is able to cover more ground in a single day or week and do so with the benefit of various giftings, personalities, and strengths of individual team members. The information will not be as thorough as longer research would provide, but the various components will be contemporary with one another rather than the non-commensurate phenomena that long-term studies often provide.

Of course, such a short-term approach has many limitations as well. The quantity versus quality argument is pertinent in the consideration of this approach. For instance, the team that is in place for only one week must work in English-speaking areas or utilize interpreters. Additionally, the team will not have the benefit of knowing the personalities, culture, or tendencies of locals to embellish or hide information in their interviews. Participant observation is limited in a one-week investigation as researchers can only observe day to day happenings and will miss any cultural festivals that occur at other times of the year

As noted earlier, the recruitment of team members is one of the keys for success with short-term, team-based ethnographic research. Team members should ideally have studied cultural anthropology, ethnographic research, intercultural communication, or related subjects. In the absence of prior education, a thorough orientation into research methods, practice in qualitative interviewing, and clear instructions regarding dos and don'ts can safeguard the process. Team members who are extroverted enough to engage in conversations and interact with strangers are essential. However, another advantage of short-term trips is that naturally shy team members often find courage to step into a more extroverted personality in the knowledge that they are only in the research context for one week. Being forward in conversation and asking questions without being offensive is not a gift possessed by all. Therefore, it is good to pair those with this gift with others who may not be as socially adept. People are often open to talk about themselves and the interviewer must be able to elicit this interest, closing with, "Whom else should I talk to for information about this?"

Basic cultural information must be obtained sooner or later, and the sooner it can be obtained the better. In one week, it is possible for a trained team of researchers to discern societal, cultural, and worldview foundations. Even wide-ranging matters such as whether the culture is patriarchal or matriarchal, the basis for marriage and kinship organizations, languages spoken, religious preferences and allegiance, industry, food, music, and clothing styles are all identifiable in a short time by utilizing the team-based research approach.

## Conclusion

Ethnographic research conducted by short-term teams is a wise stewardship of funds, a practical method for conducting research, and draws on the strengths of many individuals that may be lacking in a solo researcher. Such a model is ideal for projects within an intercultural studies major, or as a short-term mission trip. Trained research teams can be very helpful for missionaries who may not have the training or time to gather the desired research.

I have outlined first what I call the team-based categorical model. This model worked well for our research goals in small town Iqaluit. Next, I examined the geographical model and its use in a diverse urban setting. Each model has its place, strengths, and weaknesses. In short, there is still a place for long-term ethnographic research, but more and more companies, churches, and mission agencies are requesting short-term research. With the proper training and preparation, small research teams such as those described here can accomplish good research in a short time.

## Worldview Identification Worksheet

| Family | Friends | Food | Festivals | Future |
|---|---|---|---|---|
| • What does your household look like, who lives with you?<br>• What language do you speak at home?<br>• Can you marry outside your culture?<br>• What does a wedding look like?<br>• Who makes major decisions in your household?<br>• What responsibilities do your children have related to the family?<br>• What role do ancestors have in your family? | • What is it like living here? Are there many people from your culture?<br>• What parts of town do most people from your culture live in? What work do they do here?<br>• Where do you spend time with friends, what do you do?<br>• What has been your experience with Americans?<br>• How are friendships different here from your home country? | • What are your favorite foods? What do you think of the food?<br>• Does your culture have a famous dish?<br>• Are there drinks, foods or animals you avoid eating? Why?<br>• What special meals do you have at religious events?<br>• Does your culture have guidelines for who prepares food, how it is served, or what order family members eat? | • What religion is most common in your culture? Do you practice that religion?<br>• Are there special days of the year or major festivals or holidays you observe?<br>• What is the significance of each one?<br>• Are the festivals different here than in your home country? How so?<br>• Could I attend one of your festivals sometime? | • What happens after we die?<br>• How do you best prepare for death and beyond?<br>• How do you relate to your ancestors who have gone to the afterlife? Do they have influence in your life?<br>• How do you relate to god/creator?<br>• Are time and history moving from point to point or are they cyclical or circular?<br>• What are you most excited about living here? What are the biggest challenges and needs? |

# Bibliography

Alba, Richard, and Victor Nee. *Remaking the American Mainstream: Assimilation and Contemporary Immigration.* Cambridge: Harvard University Press, 2003.

Casey, Anthony, and Enoch Wan. *Church Planting among Immigrants in U.S. Urban Centers: The Where, Why, and How of Diaspora Missiology in Action.* Portland: Institute of Diaspora Studies—USA, 2014.

Do, Hien Doc. *The Vietnamese Americans: The New Americans.* Westport, CT: Greenwood, 1999.

Fetterman, David. *Ethnography: Step by Step.* 2nd ed. Thousand Oaks, CA: SAGE, 1998.

Fischer, Claude. *The Urban Experience.* 2nd ed. San Diego: Harcourt Brace Jovanovich, 1984.

"The Foreign-Born Population in the United States." https://www.census.gov/newsroom/pdf/cspan_fb_slides.pdf.

Geertz, Clifford. *The Interpretation of Cultures.* New York: Basic, 1973.

Gibson, Margaret. *Accommodation without Assimilation: Sikh Immigrants in an American High School.* Ithaca, NY: Cornell University Press, 1988.

Guest, Kenneth, and Peter Kwong. "Ethnic Enclaves and Cultural Diversity." In *Cultural Diversity in the United States: A Critical Reader*, edited by Ida Susser and Thomas Patterson, 250–66. Malden, MA: Blackwell, 2001.

Hall, Stuart. "Cultural Identity and Diaspora." In *Theorizing Diaspora: A Reader*, edited by Jana Evans Braziel and Anita Mannur, 233–46. Malden, MA: Blackwell, 2003.

Hiebert, Paul, and Eloise Hiebert Meneses. *Incarnational Ministry: Planting Churches in Band, Tribal, Peasant, and Urban Societies.* Grand Rapids: Baker, 1995.

Kwong, Peter. *The New Chinatown.* New York: Hill and Wang, 1996.

Lingenfelter, Sherwood. *Ministering Cross-Culturally: An Incarnational Model for Personal Relationships.* Grand Rapids: Baker, 2003.

Maffesoli, Michel. *The Time of the Tribes: The Decline of Individualism in Mass Society.* Translated by Don Smith. London: SAGE, 1996.

Payne, J. D. *Pressure Points: Twelve Global Issues Shaping the Face of the Church.* Nashville: Nelson, 2013.

# Bibliography

———. *Strangers Next Door: Immigration, Migration, and Mission*. Downers Grove, IL: InterVarsity, 2012.

———. *Unreached Peoples, Least Reached Places: An Untold Story of Lostness in America*. N.p.: Self-published, 2014. http://www.jdpayne.org/2014/03/03/free-ebook-unreached-peoples-least-reached-places/.

Portes, Alejandro. "Modes of Structural Incorporation and Present Theories of Immigration." In *Global Trends in Migration: Theory and Research on International Population Movements*, edited by Mary Kritz et al., 279–97. Staten Island, NY: CMS, 1981.

Radhakrishnan, Rajagopalan. "Ethnicity in an Age of Diaspora." In *Theorizing Diaspora: A Reader*, edited by Jana Evans Braziel and Anita Mannur, 119–31. Malden, MA: Blackwell, 2003.

Rubin, Herbert, and Irene Rubin. *Qualitative Interviewing: The Art of Hearing Data*. Thousand Oaks, CA: SAGE, 1995.

"Table 1." https://www.dhs.gov/immigration-statistics/yearbook/2018/table1.

"Table 25." https://www.dhs.gov/immigration-statistics/yearbook/2018/table25.

Tierney, Gerry. "Becoming a Participant Observer." In *Doing Cultural Anthropology: Projects in Ethnographic Data Collection*, edited by Michael Angrosino, 9–18. 2nd ed. Long Grove, IL: Waveland, 2007.

"United States—Foreign-Born Population Percentage by State." https://www.indexmundi.com/facts/united-states/quick-facts/all-states/foreign-born-population-percent#map.

Watters, Ethan. *Urban Tribes: Are Friends the New Family?* New York: Bloomsbury, 2003.

Zelinsky, Wilbur, and Barrett Lee. "Heterolocalism: An Alternative Model of the Sociospatial Behaviour of Immigrant Ethnic Communities." *International Journal of Population Geography* 4.4 (1998) 281–98.

Zong, Jie, and Jeanne Batalova. "International Students in the United States." https://www.migrationpolicy.org/article/international-students-united-states#CountryOrigin.

www.ingramcontent.com/pod-product-compliance
Lightning Source LLC
Chambersburg PA
CBHW051109160426
43193CB00010B/1378